WHERE
THE
EDGE
GATHERS

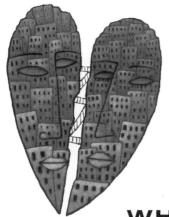

WHERE THE EDGE GATHERS

Building a Community of Radical Inclusion

Yvette A. Flunder

CLEVELAND ![ship] THE PILGRIM PRESS

The Pilgrim Press, 700 Prospect Avenue, Cleveland, Ohio 44115-1100
thepilgrimpress.com
© 2005 by Yvette A. Flunder

Printed in the United States of America on acid-free paper

10   09   08   07   06   05   5   4   3   2   1

Library of Congress Cataloging-in-Publication Data

Flunder, Yvette A.
    Where the edge gathers: building a community of radical inclusion /
Yvette A. Flunder.
        p.   cm.
    Includes bibliographical references
    ISBN 0-8298-1638-0 (pbk. : alk. paper)
    1. Community—Religious aspects—Christianity.   2. Fellowship—
Religious aspects—Christianity.   3. Reconciliation—Religious aspects—
Christianity.   I. Title.

BV625.F68   2005
253—dc22
                                                    2005047259

CONTENTS

Acknowledgments

MANY HEARTFELT THANKS are due to the folks who made up my editing team: Dr. Doris Allen, Rev. Kendal Brown, Rev. Stella "Toni" Dunbar, Ms. Emerald O'Leary, and Dr. Louis C. Knox. All of you burned the midnight oil with me and gave so much to make me look good. Thank you for helping me tell our story. I owe you chicken, the holy bird.

I also want to thank my forever family, City of Refuge United Church of Christ, for giving me time to finish this book. I missed you "muchly" when I was absent from you, and your prayers have supported me. I appreciate the stabilizing presence of all of the associate pastors. A special word of appreciation to my administrative assistants, Barbara Webb and Noni Gordon, for trying diligently to make sense of my schedule, and to Fran Houston for picking up the things I could not do and doing them without a complaint.

To my wonderful family—Shirley, my life partner, Nubian and Latrice, my girls, and Leonard, my big brother—thank you for your words of encouragement and practical advice. Shirley, I hope this is the end of the all-nighters, and I promise I will get some rest now that this drama is over. I am also blessed with the most wonderful parents in the world: Bishop James and Rt. Rev. Mother Ruth Langston. I know I scare you both sometimes, but your support of me during my many transitions is such a tangible demonstration of the love you have for me. I am your girl and I am fiercely indebted to you.

Finally, I dedicate this book to my grandparents, the late Bishop Eugene and Mother Bessie Hamilton, who first taught me to find my own voice and, by their example, showed me how to speak truth to power. Grandma and Grandpa, I know you understand it all now and I will see you in the morning.

Introduction

IN HER BOOK *Church in the Round*, Letty Russell's image of church community is a communion table around which people are seated in a circle. There is no pulpit, altar, or front or back seat. All are seated equally and everyone has equal access to the table. She calls this feminist ecclesiology or woman-church, where women and all those who have been exiled to the margin are welcome at the table. Russell emphasizes this image stating that:

> The critical principle of feminist ecclesiology is a table principle. It looks for ways that God reaches out to include all those whom society and religion have declared outsiders and invites them to gather round God's table of hospitality. The measure of the adequacy of the life of a church is how it is connected to those on the margin, whether those, as the NRSV calls "the least of these who are members of my family," are receiving the attention to their needs for justice and hope. (Matt 25:40)[1]

This "table principle" is an explicit call for the inclusion of the marginalized, and it offers a challenging notion of what it means to be a Christian community. In order to create a viable community, hospitality and inclusivity are essential. I draw on those principles and seek to extend those fruitful ideas. I believe, however, that inclusivity and hospitality must be coupled with accountability to and responsibility for the community if it is to be sustained. To that end, I offer the metaphor of village life, attempting to capture by it the dual ideas of inclusivity and accountability.

The village metaphor reflects the indigenous tribes of Africa, South America, and other parts of the world that live in villages made of dwellings that surround a central meeting place or hearth. I have visited such villages or encampments during my frequent visits to Africa. They lie both on the outskirts of cities and in the interior. A common custom in the village is to live in dwellings or kraals often without doors and to use the central hearth as the place where all are welcome. The village life is a life that balances openness and privacy. Tribes, people of Africa and South America, often have no doors on their dwellings, yet they know when and where it is appropriate to enter and exit. Nothing is hidden to the living or to the ancestors, yet everyone knows where the invisible boundaries are. I use this metaphor as a model for creating, sustaining, and celebrating Christian community among people who are marginalized by church and society and cannot or choose not to hide the cause of their marginalization.

The creation of Christian community among people marginalized by the church and society requires that the community maintain a presence of cultural familiarity while actively fighting and overcoming oppressive and exclusive theology. Sustaining community among people who visibly represent marginalized groups necessitates (a) the use of village ethics or knowing where the boundaries are when all things are exposed and (b) the importance of village table theology or giving everyone a seat at the central meeting place or the welcome table.

In this book I will use examples of persons most marginalized by church and society to illustrate the use of village ethics and theology. I will reexamine sexual and relational ethics, demonstrate the importance of radical inclusivity, and show the need to destigmatize our view of any group of people.

Finally, because visibly marginalized people are together in community does not mean that each affirms the other, or that their common marginality will hold the community together. Conversely, people who have been oppressed often learn to oppress by assimilating the oppressor in an effort to gain power and influence. There must be glue to hold the community on the margin together, something that continuously defines and strengthens the essence of the community. If community is to celebrate, it must be reminded that its existence is something to be glad about.

I suggest that preaching is one tool that defines, reinforces, and supports the collective theology of the community. Preaching tells and retells the community story. It is the primary glue that holds the fragile, fragmented, marginalized community together. Preaching in the call and response method of the black church is a circle experience. I will include sermons and stories that reinforce a theology that is radically inclusive while encouraging responsibility and accountability.

As I reflect and elaborate upon the metaphor of the village, I will draw upon my own extensive pastoral experience with marginalized people and bring that experience into critical conversation with relevant theological and pastoral literature.

I have been a pastor in the inner city for twenty years. Marginalized communities have always been overrepresented in the churches where I have served. The church where I currently pastor is predominantly African American, with roots in the Pentecostal, Baptist, and Methodist churches. Represented in our membership are persons who are recovering from substance abuse, in therapy, undocumented, physically and emotionally disabled, recently incarcerated, living with HIV/AIDS, same gender loving (SGL) persons,[2] transgendered persons, and a number of people in the helping professions who serve these populations. The people in our church who do not fit any of these categories indicate by their presence their support of people who are living on the edge of society.

VISIBILITY AND OPPRESSION

People who are not representative of a *visibly marginalized group* can remain invisible until they choose to disclose their issues, even if those issues would qualify them as part of a marginalized community. If they are on the edge, they can hide it. There are people who have issues that, if known, would make them unacceptable in their churches, their families, or their jobs, but because their issue of "unacceptability" is not visible they can keep it hidden until they choose to reveal themselves in less threatening surroundings. The disparity between people's real life stories and their outward appearance is frequently surprising.

However, many marginalized people are visible and therefore vulnerable. The visibility of the characteristic for which they are marginalized is often the cause of the marginalization. Most marginalized people, such as people of color, transgendered people, and persons with certain disabilities, cannot hide their otherness in the dominant society. There is no hiding place, no privilege of being mistaken as one who fits. One cannot maintain anonymity.

What do people do when the dominant society forces them to the margin? In order for visibly marginalized people to have real community they must develop community while exposed—naked, with their "marginality" in full view—often learning to celebrate the very thing that separates them from the dominant culture. In recent years many aboriginal and indigenous people have increased their cultural pride and identity by celebrating the way of life lived in their villages before the colonials came. On a recent trip to South Africa I was invited to a gospel music concert where a pastor joined the singers and danced in traditional Zulu dress, with his full torso and legs completely exposed. It was a powerful moment of identity for the largely Zulu audience. They had found renewed life in the very thing the colonizer called heathen, primitive, and barbaric.

Albert Memmi in his book *The Colonizer and the Colonized* refers to the colonial as a usurper, who, having come to another's land and culture, "succeeded not merely in creating a place for himself, but also in taking away that of the inhabitant, granting himself astounding privileges to the detriment of those rightfully entitled to them."[3] Memmi states further that the colonial does this, "by upsetting the established rules and substituting his own." When a people are colonized the community is destabilized and forced to accept values and exist in a paradigm foreign to it. The colonizer, by a show of force or use of religion, asserts power over those he/she seeks to control. Then the oppressor can cull a few from the colonized and teach them the art of oppressing their own for power in the new system. Generations become infected with an oppression sickness that manifests in detachment, dislocation, classism, and further marginalization.

The European explorers and missionaries who colonized Africa, Polynesia, and South America taught an enduring lesson of secret keeping. They came equipped with the skills to make clothes and doors and secrets. They did not acknowledge the great gift of village life: to know and be known, to see and be seen frees one from the preoccupation of pretense. The church of Jesus Christ has been colonized in much the same way, by a dominant culture that would change the radically inclusive ministry of Jesus into one that encourages people to seek to hide their "unacceptable" realities in order to be embraced. Adherence to the rules of the dominant culture is not freedom. Marginalized people must seek freedom from a belief that says, "There is no community outside of the dominant culture; therefore, to have community one must assimilate." External assimilation does not make one a part of community; it simply covers up our reality and gives us license to act like someone we are not. Historically, faith leaders have been a very strong voice for justice and compassion in political and social life. Faith leaders, time and again, have taken the lead and have been a voice of conscience regarding issues ranging from poverty and homelessness to peace and civil rights. However, the vast majority of churches remain extremely judgmental in their theology and conservative in their politics towards people who traditionally have lived at the margins of society.

My history and experience is in African American churches where many congregations and their leaders suffer from oppression sickness. Oppression sickness is a legacy of cultural oppression suffered by African Americans and passed down from generation to generation. Religious authorities with a history of rejection turn into oppressors by excluding and condemning those of whom they disapprove. The doctrines and tenets of Christianity currently practiced by African Americans in this country were learned in the context of chattel slavery where classism, racism, and sexism were the rule. Over time, the institution of the African American church itself has contributed to populating the margins of society by this mode of oppressive exclusion. Many African American churches have achieved substantial power and influence within their respective communities and denominations by marginalizing certain segments of society. Furthermore, this external marginalizing is often mirrored within the very structure of authority of churches, which typically are patriarchal and rigidly hierarchical.

Recently, however, there has been a growing movement to challenge the theology that allows churches to be private social clubs and calls on them to become more involved in the life of the community. This enables the celebration of diversity and inclusion of all peoples, especially those who have traditionally been marginalized by religious institutions. Yet there is often a heavy price to pay for individual pastors and their congregations who make this courageous change: congregations become bitterly divided, membership decreases, financial stability is lost, leaders are removed from their positions of authority, and social ostracism is unleashed on the pastors and their congregations alike. The end result, however, is the creation of true Christian community.

True community—true church—comes when marginalized people take back the right to fully "be." A people must be encouraged to celebrate not in spite of who they are, but because of who their Creator has made them. The balm that heals oppression sickness is the creation of accountable, responsible, visible, celebrating communities on the margin of mainline church and dominant society.

PART ONE

Community

CREATING COMMUNITY

IN HIS EFFORT to define the church of the future Loren Mead makes this statement about community:

> We need to belong—to be part of a larger world. The need to belong drives us to community, a place where we know we belong. It is also a place where we will be safe—a kind of "home base" in the world's chaotic game of "tag." It is a place where you are valued for what you are in yourself. All of this is wrapped up in the word community, and all of it is a mix of people and places, memories and values.[1]

When access to existing communities is not available, marginalized people must seek to develop community for and among themselves. Where people are giving birth to a fresh, emerging Christian community, old barriers exist and must be overcome.

OVERCOMING OPPRESSIVE THEOLOGY

The theology of those at the center of society often seeks to characterize people on the edge as enemies of God. This is especially true when individuals or groups unrepentantly refuse to conform to the dominant definition of normativeness. Overcoming internal and external oppressive theology, or a theology that excludes certain people, is primary in creating a Christian community for people visibly on the periphery. Those who promote theologies that exclude certain races, cultures, sexual and gender orientations, and classes in the name of Jesus would do well to remember that Jesus was himself from the edge of society with a ministry to those who were considered least. Jung Young Lee, describing the marginality and the ministry of Jesus, states that

> Jesus' public ministry may best be characterized as a life of marginality. He was a homeless man with a group of homeless people around him. The people Jesus called to be his disciples were marginalized people. None came from the religious establishment; they were not elders, high priests, or Judaic-law teachers. Most were fishermen, except for a tax collector and a clerk, Judas, who betrayed Jesus. His other associations were primarily with the poor, weak, outcast, foreigners, and prostitutes.[2]

Marginalized people, now as in the time of Jesus' earthly ministry, respond to a community of openness and inclusivity where other people from the edge gather. Such an atmosphere welcomes people to feel it is safer to be who they are. A liberating theology of acceptance must be embodied in the atmosphere of a liberating Christian community. Contempt for the church and all things religious often stems from exposure to oppressive theology, biblical literalism, and unyielding tradition. A person, church, or society can do extreme harm when that harm is done in the name of God and virtue and with the "support" of Scripture. In *The Good Book*, Peter Gomes reflects on an old aphorism he heard from a friend: "A surplus of virtue is more dangerous than a surplus of vice, because a surplus of virtue is not subject to the constraints of conscience."[3] Many people rejected by the church got their burns from Bible-believing Christian flamethrowers.

In the African American Metho-Bapti-Costal[4] tradition there is an example of *oppression sickness* that masquerades as virtue. The ancestors of present-day African Americans were taught to cover up in the daylight and were often sexually and physically abused behind closed doors at night. This brought about shame and guilt regarding the body, but what was worse was what went on behind those doors, under those clothes, in the dark, late at night. Africans came to realize that virtue was a white thing for white people that did not extend to the slave; the rules came in different colors. Sin and evil were black; goodness and virtue were white.

Peter Paris says of the "Christian" slave trader:

> Slave traders saw no contradiction between being Christian and being engaged in the sale of human cargo. Although Christians espoused a universal doctrine that God created all humans, their theology did not imply the equality of all humanity. On the contrary, their refusal to acknowledge the full humanity of African peoples implied the absence of any moral issue with respect to slavery. Consequently, slave traders saw no contradiction between being Christian, on the one hand, and the buying and selling of human slaves on the other hand.[5]

The slaveholders were the people who taught Africans who were brought to the Americas about Jesus, a Jesus who loved Africans as long as they were content to be slaves, a Jesus who supported the snatching of babies from their mothers' breasts and selling them down river. Good religious folks, who could sing "Amazing Grace" on the deck of a slave ship or at a burning, beating, or a lynching, were the examples of good moral Christians. John Kater in his book *Christians on the Right* is correct in his assertion that all theology serves someone. The question is whom does it serve? Who benefits and at whose expense? When we are finished cooking up and serving our theologies, who reigns and who suffers? Kater describes the state of the slaveholding religious south in this statement, "Both Jesus and the prophets before him knew well that it is possible to practice religion without seeking Justice."[6] The slave's understanding of a God who could allow such atrocities would have to be joined with internalized inferiority. This oppression is rooted deeply in the African American community's spirit. African Americans demonstrate certain characteristics of African spiritualism such as ecstatic, cathartic behavior in worship with dancing and "shouting"—behavior very similar to and central to the liturgy of West African peoples. Yet we are told what Africans do is demonic and what African Americans do is the Holy Spirit. African Americans have systematically been taught that

all indigenous African expressions of faith are heathen, demonic, or ignorant. Some African American churches refuse to sing songs with call
and response or long repeating choruses because it has been suggested
that only ignorant people sing the same thing over and over, yet the repeating chant is a significant part of our musical history.

In 1706 six colonial legislatures passed acts denying that Christian
baptism made slaves equal to whites. Their fear was that the slaves
might become "saucy" if they saw themselves equal to whites in the
sight of God. Baptism began for many with the following proclamation:

> You declare in the presence of God and before the congrega-
> tion that you do not ask for the holy baptism out of any design
> to free yourself from the Duty and Obedience that you owe
> your master while you live, but merely for the good of Your
> Soul and to partake of the Graces and Blessings promised to
> the members of the Church of Jesus Christ.[7]

Preachers allowed to preach to slaves had to constantly reinforce
and remind them that they were never going to be equal to their masters . . . not now nor in the hereafter.

A slave, Frank Roberson, paraphrased the kind of preaching slaves
were subjected to:

> You will go to heaven if you are good, but don't ever think that
> you will be close to your mistress and master. No! No! There
> will be a wall between you; but there will be holes in it that
> will permit you to look out and see your mistress when she
> passes by. If you want to sit behind this wall, you must do the
> language of the text "Obey your masters."[8]

In order to even preach to the slaves the preacher had to convince the
slaveholder that Christianity would produce a more docile, obedient slave.

It is impossible to come into the Christian faith through the slave
door and not have a skewed view of relationship with the Creator and a
sideways interpretation of virtue. According to M. Shawn Copeland,

> Black women's suffering redefined caricatured Christian
> virtues. Because of the lives and suffering of Black women

held in chattel slavery—the meanings of forbearance, long-suffering, patience, love, hope, and faith can never again be ideologized. Because of the rape, seduction, and concubinage of Black women under chattel slavery, chastity or virginity begs new meaning.[9]

Just as child abuse passes from one generation to the next, so does spiritual/theological abuse, and the resulting contagious oppression sickness can make the oppressed a "virtuous" oppressor. Oppression sickness is internalized oppression that causes the oppressed to be infected by the sickness of the oppressor. The effort to mimic the dominant Christian culture or those "truly favored" by God has greatly infected the African American church tradition with classism, sexism, heteroprivilege, patriarchy, and closed doors. How does an inferior-feeling group of people feel superior? By finding someone else to make inferior. Accordingly, light-colored people feel superior to dark people. Educated people feel superior to undereducated people. Men lord over women. Delores S. Williams in her critique of James Cone's groundbreaking book, *A Black Theology of Liberation,* reveals that although the book became "scripture for many black seminarians who had for years been trying to reconcile their own black experience of Jesus in the black Christian community with the Jesus they met in Eurocentric theological education," it fell woefully short of addressing the "horrible exploitation black women have experienced in both the black and white worlds."[10]

The "haves" continue to lord over the "have nots." Straight people bash SGL people. Elias Farajaje-Jones, in his essay "Breaking Silence," says,

Many Black people believe it is acceptable to be openly homophobic/biphobic. The Black Church definitely encourages this through words and actions. Indeed, expressing homophobia/biphobia to reaffirm their heterosexual privilege is often the only situation in which many Black Christians feel that they have any form of privilege at all.[11]

The pulpit often becomes a place of monarchy, not ministry, particularly when the pulpit is the only place where the minister has value. Whoever is considered the "Gentile" in our midst is often oppressed. Some African Americans who got their opportunity to succeed through affirmative action speak against it, forgetting that colored people were lynched fighting for it. In *Shades of Freedom*, A. Leon Higginbotham refers to such an elitist attitude among African American professionals in a scathing critique of Supreme Court Justice Clarence Thomas. He states, "Many white judges share an underlying belief about the rarity of racist occurrences in the courtroom. In contrast, I know of only one African American Federal Judge (Thomas) who minimizes the significance of the fact that societal racism, even unintentional, often affects the adjudicatory and fact-finding process of court."[12] In *Reflections of an Affirmative Action Baby*, lawyer and author Stephen Carter comments that there are no black conservatives, only neoconservatives whose only claim to blackness is their skin, and who have forgotten their roots.[13]

The African village concept of community was demonized along with African religion; so much was lost in the crossing of the Atlantic. When a low sense of self-worth is present it often seems necessary to stand tall on someone else's back. In the world of church, regardless of the ethnicity or culture, those backs often belong to the people who do not fit—the ones who are obviously, visibly "other." This is a peculiar paradox, as the African American church has a long history of fighting for the rights of those in its pews and community.

For more than four hundred years, the African American church has been the principle source of sanctuary, education, socialization, information, and community for people of African descent in this country. Most of the great African American civil rights leaders, for example, Martin Luther King Jr., Barbara Jordan, Rosa Parks, and Jesse Jackson, are products of the black church, yet this black church community that endured so much oppression during its development on the margin has become an oppressor for many.

In *Unrepentant, Self–Affirming, Practicing*, Gary Comstock reveals the findings of Michael Dickens's survey of SGL men of African descent in Connecticut. Dickens acknowledges the leading role of the black church in "all progressive changes in civil rights since the days of slavery," yet he says, "When we realize the important contribution the black church has made, we begin to understand how truly devastating it is for someone to be condemned for their homosexuality by an institution that has long been in the vanguard of the cause of Justice."[14] In order to create community among people on the margin, it is essential to adopt a theology that seeks to identify and eradicate oppression sickness no matter what the root cause may be.

Oppressive theology, or a theology that welcomes those who fit a normative definition of the dominant culture while excluding those who do not, is a ball and chain on the heart of the body of Christ, and with it we keep each other in bondage. The church of Jesus Christ is in the midst of change, not all of it for the better. Any theology that suggests that God receives some and rejects others is not reflective of the ministry of Jesus Christ. Comstock insists that "the church has simply gone astray from a basis, center, origin in a common carpenter who welcomed, included, and healed the broken, outcast, and needy."[15] Jesus established the role of ministry that was being ushered in by the phenomenon of God being made flesh when Jesus read from the scroll of Isaiah one Sabbath morning. Jesus said the Spirit of the Sovereign God was upon him for this purpose to:

> Preach good tidings to the meek
> Bind up the broken-hearted
> Proclaim liberty to the captives
> Open the prison to them that are bound
> Proclaim the acceptable year [the year of Jubilee]
> Comfort all that mourn
> Give beauty for ashes and the oil of joy for mourning
> Give a garment of praise for the spirit of heaviness
> Make us trees of righteousness, plantings of God.
>
> (Isa. 61:1–3; Luke 4:18, 19 adapted from KJV)

These priorities must also be the priorities of an oppression-free Christian community. How can we be the church of Jesus unless we reflect the ministry of Jesus? Is the church a radical incarnation of the ministry of Jesus or a private social club? It is crucial in the formation of community that those who were and are oppressed seek to overcome the theological millstones tied around their necks. It is equally important to eschew pejorative assumptions toward others in community who are different to avoid passing on the sickness of oppressive theology. This inherited oppression leads to stereotyping for the purpose of gaining power or advantage.

Donald Chinula, using Martin Luther King Jr.'s notion of the "beloved community," asserts that oppression manifested as an unjust use of authority or advantage "seeks its own advantage at the expense of the oppressed and strives to perpetuate itself."[16] Stereotyping allows the oppressor to stand apart from the oppressed and categorize and pigeonhole a group of people. This oppression is particularly insidious when the Bible is used to defend it. Chinula says, "Women are oppressed because they happen to be women. This is invidious stereotyping. It is the perpetuation of a belief that a person or a group possesses characteristics or qualities that typify that group, and the use of that belief against its members."[17] This cycle of naming and blaming marginalized people has historically been the biblically based justification of the violence perpetrated against individuals, races, and nations.

The principal message that goes out from the church of Jesus Christ should declare, "Freedom in Christ is freedom in life—*all are welcome at the table.*"

INTIMACY WITH GOD

Creating community with and among marginalized people who have been alienated from the Christian community must include encouragement to seek an intimate relationship with God. An assurance of relationship with God provides the security to interpret critically the scriptures and traditions that have alienated so many for so long. People on the edge must be encouraged to form a concept of a loving God who desires to have intimate relationship with his/her creation. This must precede a historical/critical analysis of Scripture. Having a secure location in God makes it permissible to question those passages of Scripture that have traditionally brought terror. A woman minister, a SGL person, or the progeny of slaves cannot be a biblical literalist. It would be entirely too difficult to explain away all of the texts that do not support her personhood and her call. Where, then, is the place of the Bible in the life of the marginalized church? My position is best explained by a response from an unnamed slave who, when she was told that the Bible said she was to be a slave, answered, "Not my Bible; I tore dat page out!"

True spiritual liberation is the Spirit of God working in our spirits, revealing God to us. There is a danger in making the Bible God, instead of seeing the Bible as writings that point to God. According to Gomes, when we seek to interpret the Bible we should be careful of these things:

> Bibliolatry or the worship of the Bible, making of it an object of veneration and ascribing to it the glory due to God. Literalism or the worship of the text in which the letter is given, is an inappropriate superiority over the spirit, and culturism or the worship of the culture, in which the Bible is forced to conform to the norms of the prevailing culture.[18]

As to the issue of culturism, in this country we often hear "God is the God of our America. We are the people God loves most. Let's get America back to God." It is as though we have an exclusive right to God. In our nation, what is called Christianity is often Americanism. "God must prefer my country because I do." With this thinking, we can close the borders to aliens, oppress minorities, justify foreign wars, continue manifest destiny, or whatever because "God is our God and prefers us." In his discourse about "nation worship," Kater asks the question, "Is it really appropriate to consider ourselves the Chosen People and the successor among the nations, of God's Promised Land? Is it not more a sign of that pride that the Bible considers a temptation?"[19]

Certain political parties and special interest groups think God belongs to them. You can hear language about God coupled with everything from the political agenda of the religious right to the gun lobby. Similarly, African Americans and other minorities sometimes feel God loves us much more than anyone else and that we are sanctified by our history of suffering.

Making God the sole property of certain nations and cultures leads us to making God the sole property of denominations, each one claiming sole proprietorship of the truth. Within the Christian church, we teach baptism in Jesus' name, in the names of the trinity as well as for adults only, for children only, by immersion, by sprinkling, as necessary for salvation, and as a prerequisite for the gift of the Holy Spirit. Who is right?

Turf wars abound for ownership of the "real word" of God. The division this causes is amazing. God is not exclusively the God of any nation, or any denomination. Nations are formed to facilitate the needs of their citizens. Christian denominations are set up to facilitate the work of the church on earth. People—individuals, not buildings or institutions—are called to be a habitation for the Spirit of God. It is intimacy with God that emboldens people in their quest to extricate life-giving principles from the Bible.

I would like to argue for one other reason to encourage people to seek intimacy with God as a prerequisite to a critical study of Scripture. I call it preconceived interpretation.

PRECONCEIVED INTERPRETATION

Most people who have been impacted by society and the traditions of the church will go to the Bible reasonably sure of what it says about major issues, without a critical analysis of what the Bible does say. We have been taught historically that God is for this and against that, and we approach Scripture expecting to find those passages that defend the culturally accepted position. A historical/cultural understanding of what God "requires" is very difficult to uproot.

Historically and culturally accepted views that have been defended with Scripture include teachings against interracial marriage, against women ministers, against SGL people, against working mothers, and more. The Bible has also been used to defend war, slavery, and the death penalty. These beliefs are the foundation of our nation, our culture, and many of our faith communities. It takes a great deal of security for a theologically abused person to come to the study of Scripture seeking to understand the times, context, politics, culture, religion, and social norms represented by the thousands of years of history in the Bible.

Learning new ways to look at Scripture, no matter how liberating, can be a threat to one's foundation. Learning also involves unlearning deeply rooted principles. This is particularly challenging for people who have already suffered great loss. The security to meet this challenge comes from understanding that we know and are known by God.

CULTURAL IDENTITY AND VULNERABILITY

There is a concern that must be addressed here and a question that I am often asked. "If we resist the result of oppression sickness that was handed down to us and made us feel rejected by the church and just barely received by God, if we dispel that defeatist thinking, will we retain the atmosphere, style, sound, and feel of the church as we know it?" In my experience, I have found it is quite possible to have the style, sound, and feel of the Metho-Bapti-Costal church without the oppression perpetuated by some in these traditions.

The preaching, the song, and the dance are media through which the Spirit moves; *they are ours*, and they should remain. God can move through any culture. When Mercy Amba Oduyoye, a Ghanaian womanist theologian, was challenged in a class I took from her about the church in Africa demonstrating too much traditional African spirituality, she said, "The Owner of the church will purify and use it as he sees fit." It is not necessary to choose between a Spirit-filled oppressive church and a cold, dead, liberated church. Church can be very effervescent and joyful while simultaneously being theologically liberating, justice oriented, culturally appropriate, and inclusive.

Often when someone is introduced to the possibility of being accepted in a Christian community, after being rejected for so long, there is a period of what I call cathartic vulnerability. During this time, people take every opportunity to tell their story, a story that has possibly been bottled up for years. Stories of oppression, fear, guilt, self-hatred, survival, and hope surface. People compare scars. When the stories begin to flow out of one experience to another, and from one person to another, similarities begin to emerge around which people can identify and community forms. Community then is a circle of open huts around a central welcoming table where everyone has a place to come to be healed. There is no more need to put forth a pathetic half-hearted effort to be accepted; an individual's seat at the table is not given *in spite of* who they are but *because of* who they are.

The reality of having a seat at the table and knowing a great deal about each other's lives, however, does not imply that the community is healthy or that each person's damage is healed. There are great challenges in the life of a community where people with multiple levels of pain, loss, and crisis come together. The created community must be sustained.

Sustaining Community

WHILE CREATING COMMUNITY among marginalized people centers on a common need for acceptance and affirmation, sustaining community is quite another matter. In order for peace and order to exist in the village there must be a way to be, together. It is often difficult for people who have not had full rights to community life to understand that freedom without responsibility and accountability is as detrimental as slavery. Freedom cannot be an end unto itself. Freedom from something must flow into freedom to be something else or it is not truly freedom. The object of *getting* free is *being* free: the object of *being* free is *living* free.

Martin Luther states that the true freedom of the Christian comes from faith in Christ and love for our neighbor. In describing the "free" Christian community he says, "Christians live not in themselves, but in Christ and in their neighbors. Otherwise they are not Christians. They live in Christ through faith and in their neighbor through love."[1] If we are free from evil, hatred, and dysfunction, we are constrained to help establish the beloved community, where all can live free.

In order for a community to thrive, there must be an understanding of faithful community-building behavior and a disseminating of duties and chores. Faithful community-building behavior suggests that each member of the community concerns him-/herself with the effect of her/his behavior on the good of the community. The dissemination of duties and chores ensures that all members share in and contribute to the welfare of the community.

There must also be respect for understood boundaries. In the village there are no doors on the huts, but one must know when it is intrusive to enter, and even though clothing is minimal, one must know the rules of touching and staring. Although all are welcome at the table, a certain behavior is expected.

Additionally, sustaining Christian community requires an intentional effort to design a framework that includes everyone in the life of the church. We must constantly revisit the commitment to be inclusive and compassionate along with being responsible and accountable. Sustaining community in an atmosphere of openness and mutual vulnerability requires a conscientious look at village ethics for a people whose common denominator is oppression, but whose lives and lifestyles may differ greatly. The idea about village ethics of a straight person who has been incarcerated, or a mother who has a history of drug use, may be very different than those of an SGL youth or person living with AIDS. Finding common ethical ground is as important to the survival of the community as the theology of the welcoming table is to the creation of community.

I will lift up some ethical, pastoral, and ecclesiological considerations for sustaining community on the margin and some additional recommendations for community life.

MARRIAGES AND UNIONS

Sexual ethics and boundaries are essential to the health of the community because the definition of ethical sexual practice differs significantly from one individual to another. While volumes have been written about heterosexual marriage, very little has been written regarding sexual ethics for SGL Christians and couples. The family, straight or SGL, is an integral part of the church community. Defining family for SGL Christians is a struggle in itself as family units other than the heterosexual norm are just now truly emerging; however, the stability of family relationships is foundational to the stability of the community. According to Kater,

What this means for twentieth-century Christians is that we cannot hope to fulfill the Biblical demands for justice and love by imitating the social institutions of twenty centuries ago, but are called instead to examine our own institutions and mores in the light of the City of God. Marriage is Christian, not when it conforms to law, from which we have been set free, but when it becomes a sacrament.[2]

How should the church respond to families that do not fit the acceptable social norm? When is marriage a sacrament? The Christian church had a similar dilemma two hundred years ago when it sought to determine how to justify the inclusion of slave families that did not fit the requirement set forth by the church. Some churches as far back as the 1800s had decided to conditionally welcome slaves as members. The issue was how could the church receive them "in good standing" when some of the married slaves had both their current spouses and another spouse and often other children on another plantation. This was due in large part to the ability of the slave master to sell slaves away at will. Underlying this issue was the fact that slave marriages were not considered valid and legal, as slaves were not truly "people," but possessions. How could the church make their marriages sacred and make them accountable to their vows if their master could force them in and out of their marriages? One church, the Welsh Neck Baptist Church of South Carolina, decided that to grant membership to the slave couples was "less evil" than excommunicating them. It further stated:

> That servants separated by their owners, & removed to too great a distance to visit each other, may be considered dead to each other; & therefore at liberty to take a second companion, in the lifetime of the first; as the act of separation was not their own voluntary choice; but the will of those who had legal control over them.[3]

This forward-thinking group of Christians was able to see beyond the religious legalism of their time and find a way to help these families so different from their own.

Good sound relationships are foundational in the formation of families. But what is a family? In my history and in the experience of the

African American community, it was often not nuclear and was not typified by the television programs of my youth—*Donna Reed, Leave It to Beaver,* or *Father Knows Best.* I relate to Michael Piazza, pastor of Cathedral of Hope Metropolitan Community Church, who said, "We live in a world where families are as diverse as the people who inhabit them. Family values must mean more than living in the suburbs with 2.4 kids, a large screen TV, and a thirty-year mortgage."[4]

Aunts, grandparents, family friends, and nonrelatives raised many of my friends. I, like many others, am the product of a broken home, but it did not seem broken, as the village/church was so familylike. We were in a community where the adults were responsible for everyone's children and we as children were responsible to the adults who cared for us.

Some definition and affirmation must be given to same-sex couples to establish beginning points for relationship accountability to and from the community. Relationships must be established in some way to indicate clearly what the expectations are for the church, the extended family, parents, children, and former significant others.

Same-sex unions should not only be an acceptable practice in the Christian church, but these unions are essential to the harmony of the church community where SGL parishioners are present. These unions are essential for the support of couples who have so few examples of sexual fidelity and long-term commitment.

In my pastoral experience, I have been involved with ministries where there were large numbers of SGL African American persons. These ministries often placed a major emphasis on music and other forms of artistic expression. I have seen the theological and doctrinal positions of these churches change progressively as they sought to include SGL persons who were integral to the life of the community.

It seems difficult in most cases, however, to cross the line from benevolent tolerance to full affirmation; to create a community of affectional orientation parity along with gender parity, class parity, and the like. The struggle seems to be centered on finding a socially acceptable, normative, and safe way to fully incorporate homosexual parishioners, alongside straight parishioners. What does a predominantly straight ministry do with its SGL parishioners, without offending the straight folks?

What has occurred is a subculture of SGL persons in the Christian community who are not necessarily condemned for being SGL, but who are also not given equal status with heterosexual persons in a heteronormative environment. SGL Christians are not often free to celebrate anniversaries, be close in public, or share a last name. Marriage and relationship seminars and "how to" workshops are often limited to heterosexual couples. Betty Berzon, in her book *Permanent Partners*, suggests that heterosexual couples expect permanence in their partnerships because the structures of extended family and the legal system built around their relationships reinforce their permanence.[5] "Gay and Lesbian people, on the other hand, tend to approach their partner relationships with the hope that these will be long-lasting, even though the prospect is largely unconfirmed by their own experience, and that of most of the people they know."[6]

In the same way that little attention was given to the "invalid" marriages of slave couples, little attention is given to developing same-sex families. SGL couples are not challenged to answer the hard questions regarding commitment—to do so would validate an invalid marriage. Even in theologically liberal environments this model seems to give a message that says, "If you are SGL we accept you, without any accountability, just to let you know how inclusive and gracious we are; but we hold straight Christians to a higher moral standard." In an ethical sense, this is still second-class treatment and a step below full acceptance of SGL people into the church community. The ethicist Robert Bellah noted this second-class treatment in relationship to African Americans and Native Americans in this country: "There is first the assertion that a certain group of people lacks the qualities that would allow its members as individuals to rise and then there is the systematic deprivation of that group of all the resources necessary for its members indeed to rise."[7]

When visible SGL persons are not held accountable for faithfulness in personal relationships or held to a "standard" of moral requirements for leadership, they are not considered strong candidates for certain roles within the church. Interestingly, these roles are most often the roles that strongly impact the social norms of the community—that is, pastor, teacher, deacon, youth leader, and similar roles. In order to make all privileges and opportunities available to all persons, responsibilities, requirements, and expectations should also be equal. For example, where there is strong emphasis placed on counseling and preparation before, and support and accountability during marriage, there should be a similar means by which SGL persons can have their relationships accepted and part of church community life. I believe same sex unions would do a great deal to bring about equality.

SECOND-CLASS CITIZENSHIP

In *Professional Ethics*, Karen Lebacqz suggests that we should not only be virtuous, honest, and trustworthy in our actions, but that our doing honorable things should be reflective of our being honorable persons.[8] If a person feels forced to live a secret life in order to sustain an intimate relationship and simultaneously be accepted by a beloved community, how can that person be internally honorable? Life then becomes a web of lies, disjointed and lacking integration. After a period of time, the life story becomes one of survival deception, and the person becomes a deceiver in order to survive in the community. Lebacqz says, "When we act, we not only do something, we also shape our own character. Our choices about what to do are also choices about who to be."[9]

The SGL Christian's life becomes a self-fulfilling prophecy; the accusation is that there is something secret going on, and sure enough there is. How can it be possible for SGL Christians to move to a place of trustworthiness if there is no framework in which to come forward and be honest? It is the inaccessibility of first-class opportunity that creates a second-class subculture. The opportunity to demonstrate capability, competence, and commitment is overshadowed by a negative perception that demonizes, even amidst an atmosphere of tolerance; a perception that says "this person is not really capable of lofty ideals . . . this person's character is automatically flawed, by virtue of his or her being SGL, and we will not allow him or her an opportunity to prove otherwise!"

I find it alarming that many who suspect the entire SGL community of being severely promiscuous also resist normalizing SGL monogamous unions. This lose-lose situation will in time do great harm to a person's self-esteem and does cause many individuals to seek clandestine, anonymous intimate encounters in order to live out their sexuality while staying in a place of guarded acceptance by the church. In this age of AIDS, the church ought to be more concerned than any other institution on earth about the prima facie duty to do no harm. The church must remove the pejorative assumptions regarding SGL people and provide equal access and equal opportunity for full participation.

Integrity is the way our lives fit together in some orderly sensible fashion, implying predictability and continuity. It is impossible to live an integrated life and simultaneously have something as important as a committed love relationship that must be perpetually hidden from the community of faith. William N. Eskridge in *The Case for Same-Sex Marriage* says that such unions "civilize" relationships.[10] When I first read this word in relationship to SGL unions I was offended. After reading further I understood Eskridge's position and have listed some of the "civilizing" aspects of same–sex unions.

The law currently makes intimacy between same-sex people a criminal offense in some states; hence legal same-sex unions would legitimize intimacy. Same- sex unions would offer an alternative to the exaggerated benefit of promiscuity, which according to Eskridge has not been liberating to SGL men, and has encouraged a cult of youth and beauty worship and the spread of sexually transmitted diseases. Unions would provide a more stable environment where children are present.

It is important that I acknowledge the opinion of those who feel this position is restrictive and limiting and that what I am suggesting seeks to, in Eskridge's words, "tame" the same-sex community.

There are SGL persons who think same-sex unions are simply a parody of heterosexual marriage and resist the notion of state recognized unions. They do not consider monogamy a viable option, and not everyone is interested in connecting to a community. I do not believe it is just for coupled people to enjoy insurance, tax, and housing benefits not available to single people or people whose intimate circles are made up of more than two persons. Some individuals are more suited to and even called to single life. Some are bisexual and live in intimate circles of mutual respect, love, and understanding. I do not seek to demonize or vilify any people or any family, but rather I seek to demonstrate that it is just and right for church and society to support and affirm same-sex couples, thereby providing a long-term relationship option for those who feel such an option is impossible.

LONE WOLF ALTERNATIVE

Some of my sisters and brothers feel that a full, unrestricted freedom for sexual intimacy between consenting adults is much more liberating and such freedom should not be accountable to the community by respecting existing relationship boundaries. I call this a lone wolf alternative where connections and relationships shift and change according to present feelings and without regard to commitments made, leaving enormous emotional and spiritual damage in its wake. There is great division in the SGL community around this issue. Although I do not seek to judge the rightness or wrongness of these opposing viewpoints, I have found it extremely difficult to experience sustained harmony in a church community where the lone wolf ideal prevails and where existing relationships are not honored.

By the "lone wolf" I mean that there are individuals who choose to move alone, not apparently connected to any one person for any length of time, actively seeking intimate sexual relationships throughout the community with various people, including those in relationships and perhaps with inappropriate persons such as underage youth. Sexual addiction is also a reality in all communities. Linda Handel in her discussion of sex addictions states that for the addict, "sex becomes confused with nurturing and caring because we live in a sexualized society where sex is confused with love."[11] She further states, "Another belief of sex addicts is that if they become dependent or committed in a relationship, their needs will not be met."[12] There are also couples who would rather not have the community involved in or aware of their relationships. In either case, there is virtually no relationship accountability to the larger community or opportunities for support. Often this is due to and born out of a history of not being accepted by the church, which results in a belief that same-sex relationships are not genuine and a desire to keep church and personal relationships separate. However, since these persons are within the community these relationships cannot be kept separate from the community, and the ebb and flow in the lives of each individual affects the community. Although these persons may seek to design a kind of relationship that keeps the church from doing them harm, it also prohibits true community involvement. While "moving alone" might function well where community is not present, opportunities for accountability are necessary for the cohesiveness of community. However, if the community does not support some affirmation of same-sex unions and other forms of family, how can same-sex people be expected to be accountable and how can those outside of these relationships respect the union?

I believe these opportunities for accountability should begin with respect for personal relationships and move out into other units such as committees, auxiliaries, councils, and the like. Fidelity is a learned behavior. I consider unions an opportunity for accountability for same-sex couples. Unclear personal commitments in any group cause blurred boundaries, thereby creating a great potential for inappropriate advances and behaviors. Preoccupation with these "affairs of the heart" hinders the work of the church and fragments the community.

In *Personal Commitments*, Margaret Farley lifts up the need for community involvement in strengthening our personal relationships. She asserts that any commitment is made stronger when there is some kind of communal support; our doubts are soothed, we are validated, our intentions are confirmed, our memories are more real, and we can get through the tough times when we know there are people alongside our relationship.[13] Additionally, community is something to which a couple can mutually attend other than themselves, to keep their lives from becoming constricted. Living in community also ensures that we will leave a legacy—a difficult thing to do from a hiding place. It is essential that the church, as community, welcome and affirm same-sex unions, to heal some of the damage of the past (damage that has resulted in an internalized fear of exposure and vulnerability) and to create possibilities for accountability and involvement in community.

THE ROLE OF THE CHURCH

It is a blessing to see the church in its role as a harbinger of justice in the presence of an unjust society. However, on the issue of same-sex unions, we must deal with the policies that structure society and the church, which influence the definition of moral correctness. This is particularly true because the majority population of both is heterosexual, fearful of the "other," and threatened by a possible negative economic impact resulting from equal rights for same-sex couples. Reinhold Neibuhr asserts in *Moral Man and Immoral Society* that the larger society, when functioning as society, is not moved by love to respond justly. Individuals who are challenged on a one-to-one basis by real and familiar people are more apt to do the right thing.[14] Neibuhr claims that our social life reveals the limit of our sympathy. Hiding in the larger society does make us less personally responsible. Consequently, when the issue of same-sex unions is considered in small close circles, acceptance and affirmation come more easily. For example, I believe that many clergy and politicians would support SGL unions if they were engaged in an intimate conversation with friends; but in the nation and church our social ego, politics, and fear do overwhelm our compassion and discernment. Whatever is the way of the majority becomes the master narrative; everything else is a "lifestyle" and deemed to be of lesser value.

Additionally, it is the desire for power in our society that often votes in the secret of the voting booth—each person seeking what will benefit him/her most and give him/her the most power and privilege. The fact that propositions 187 and 209 passed in California is evidence of this.[15] The economic implications of same-sex unions alone, for example, lower income taxes collected and greater strain on the social security budget, will probably delay the majority of Americans from voting to make same-sex unions legal.

The church, however, has a higher obligation to treat this as a justice issue. The church is to be the reflection of God, and has historically used its unique position in society to effect change in social justice issues. These issues have included abolishing slavery, securing the right to vote for women, promoting civil rights for former slaves, and ending apartheid in South Africa. This is a justice issue. Carolyn Lochhead writes

> (Heterosexual) Marriage, many gay leaders now insist, is the most obvious and profound form of state discrimination against gays and lesbians. An entire body of law hinges on the marriage contract, they argue, and with it an entire body of rights that constitute the essence of legal bias against homosexuals—from property rights to hospital-visitation privileges —as well as a deeply felt social validation.[16]

The church must, as Niebuhr encourages, meet power with power by speaking up and decrying the irrational policies that are being promoted to allegedly "protect" the institution of marriage. In *The Good Society*, Bellah et al. answer the question, "How does the Church help to right institutional wrongs?"[17] We can fulfill and build on Martin Luther King Jr.'s notion of the beloved community where "our loyalties transcend our race, our tribe, our class and our nation and people are not judged by the color of their skin [or their affectional orientation], but by the content of their character."[18] The answers given by Bellah apply to the unique role of the church in society and how that role can help to bring justice to the present political climate surrounding same sex unions:

The church's loyalty to God is above patriotism and that loyalty is what has lifted blind spots from the eyes of the church in the past. The real question should not be, "What does the majority want?" but rather, "Is there a word from God?"

The church forces individuals into a larger unit. The church brings individuals and individual thought into community. This creates the possibility of meaningful dialogue, collective prayer, and greater access to sharing available information.

The church is a principal bearer of education. The African American church, along with many other faith communities, has been a venue for education and information for hundreds of years. This education and information is not limited to religion, but includes health issues, politics, and community life. The church is a primary vein to the heart of the community.

The church teaches the Bible. Biblical religion raises questions of morality. Here is the crux of the matter for the church. What does the Bible say about same-sex unions? The answer is: *absolutely nothing.* There are texts that refer to homoeroticism and genital expression in idol worship, but even a tortured anti-SGL interpretation of these texts cannot be our principal source to determine the right or wrong of same-sex unions. More importantly, the Bible does speak clearly to the larger issues of how to treat our neighbor, the nature of commitment/covenant, and the character of the Christian community.[19]

There are many other sources that confirm the viability of same-sex unions—experienced couples, other cultures and traditions (for example, First Nations' two-spirit people). More and more books are being written that build and support these unions.

The church of Jesus Christ has a responsibility to take the lead in providing a safe home for its SGL children and to advocate for changes in the national referendum.

THE NEW ARCHE

A new arche (Middle English word that means chief, highest, most important), a higher guiding principle, a new master narrative must be instituted by, for, and in the church. This new arche must reverberate into society. I agree with Sharon Welch's position regarding the response that liberation theologians are requiring the church to signal that more has taken place than a mere acknowledgement of the Christian tradition of oppression. It is time for "repentance and conversion."[20] I feel so strongly that it is time for change that I find myself recommending two things to those seeking to have their unions sanctioned by their faith community— join supportive communities and read the Bible with liberation lenses.

Join Supportive Communities

As we are still a good distance from changing the systemic prejudice against SGL people, Farley's position on the need to change the framework of a relationship in order to keep the original meaning of the commitment certainly applies here. Persons seeking community support should go where that support is evident. Vote with your feet. Abuse is free on the street; there is no point seeking it out and joining it. We join faith communities to be strengthened and nurtured and to have an opportunity to serve. When these goals are no longer attainable, we should look elsewhere.

Read the Bible with Liberation Lenses

Mary Ann Tolbert suggests, in her essay "Reading for Liberation" that the biblically oppressed should disconnect from those biblical texts that steal freedom and personhood.[21] We must read the Bible with liberation lenses. We must look deeply for themes that affirm and set us free.

It is essential that the Christian church fully affirm the unions of SGL Christians so as to influence the next generation with the normativeness of the presence of SGL leadership and same-sex families. Forced second-class citizenship is a justice issue, an institutionalized prison that traps SGL people in an enforced deviant position if they want to remain active in the Christian community. SGL Christians cannot stay "single" without being suspected of extraordinary promiscuity, and they often cannot be united as couples in the church, as it is not permitted. Without communities to support healthy relationships, dissonant, lone wolf types who need support are more likely to reject it in favor of anonymity.

The presence of the AIDS epidemic and the recent "media sensationalism" of homosexuality has brought about some reexamination regarding the question of monogamous and committed same-sex relationships. Although the AIDS epidemic has surely made a contribution to the desire for safer-sex practices, most SGL Christians are experiencing something deeper than fear of AIDS as a catalyst for change. It is more of a metamorphosis, similar to what happens after a long revolutionary battle, when the dust settles and a new nation is born. The SGL revolution spawned a community that is now looking for a life that is less thrilling and more fulfilling.

Many SGL Christians view having multiple sex partners and anonymous, almost predatory sex as an unacceptable lifestyle. Bishop John Spong suggests that "all forms of heterosexual behavior do not receive approval. Any sexual behavior can be destructive, exploitative, predatory, or promiscuous, and therefore evil, regardless of the sexes of the parties involved."[22]

Some homosexual and heterosexual youth are making decisions to avoid the "sins" of the generation before them. There are those who agree with Theodore Walker's statement: "It is more likely that closed and committed relations are very natural and more easily learned by those who have had less opportunity to acquire the contrary experiences and habits of our more 'mature' generations. . . . (We) find that such habits, once acquired, are difficult to break."[23]

The questions I hear most often are "How does commitment or marriage work for SGL Christians?" "Should these unions be based on the heterosexual monogamous model?" and "Should we come out about our relationship and risk being stereotyped, or stay closeted and be dishonest about who we really are?" Most of my counselees are concerned with the transitory nature of most SGL relationships. Rev. Robert Williams correctly states:

> A Christian marriage is not just a random pairing of two people; it involves an intentional, well thought out, formal commitment to each other. One of the biggest problems among Gay and Lesbian couples is that since they do not have structures, such as marriage ceremonies and licenses, to mark the beginning of their relationships, they tend to slide into them without much intentionality or consciousness about the parameters of the relationship they are creating. Then, a few months or a few years down the road, they may find that their assumptions about the rules of the relationship clash with their partner's assumptions. What if one of them becomes seriously ill? What if one dies—what financial arrangements do they need to make? What if one's elderly mother wants to come live with them? What if one is offered an excellent job on the other coast; would the other quit her job to go along?[24]

I agree with Rev. Williams, who further claims that, "A Christian marriage (Gay or straight) necessarily includes elements of companionship, mutuality, commitment, and sex."[25]

Finally, leadership must come from the church; the church should be first in justice, not a back-seat driver to Canadian, Hawaiian, Vermont, or New Jersey courts or the Disney Corporation. The church should be self-critical and reexamine the call to love our neighbor as we love ourselves. If we cannot do that, we have missed our call. Tolerance must move to acceptance, acceptance to affirmation, and affirmation to celebration. Thus, my first proposal for sustaining community on the margin is that the church must give full status as well as full responsibility to all families in the community, especially those most marginalized. My second is that we must include transgendered persons into the full life of the church.

TRANSGENDERED PERSONS

An authentic ethic of inclusion must reach from the center to the farthest margin and work its way back. When we reach for the ones who are the least accepted, we give a clear message of welcome to everyone. Jesus modeled this type of radical inclusivity when he openly received those most despised by society and the religious establishment.

The transgendered community is on the edge of the edge. The church must be a sanctuary for members of the transgendered community because most of society has cast them off completely. This community of persons who live their lives opposite of their birth gender is among the least understood on the margin of church and society; in the African American faith community they are truly objects of disdain.

The church's treatment of transgendered persons is an authentic example of how oppression sickness manifests. Gordene Mackenzie takes exception with "material-based mainstream American culture" that says, "Gender behavior is usually dictated by sexual anatomy." She believes there is a spiritual dimension to gender that is not limited by "the anatomical sex assignment at birth."[26]

After a number of years working closely with the transgender community, I believe there are great lessons to be learned. It is disingenuous when the African American faith community perpetuates the cycle of oppression and particularly gender oppression by marginalizing the transgender community. The trans community makes us tell the truth about the blurred gender lines that have always existed in our community. Transgenders make us honest. We have always had manly women and womanly men in our community, who often did not identify as SGL people.

Women and men often crossed the stereotypical role lines in families, church, and community. Most people were not found on the extreme end of either masculinity or femininity, but none of us admitted it or acknowledged it. There were roles in the church for "softer" men, such as the usher board, the choir, the pulpit, or working with small children. These men often adored their wives while some wives spent most of their time with another female friend. There were roles for stronger women such as jail ministers, foreign missionaries, and trustees. People found their way into roles that complemented their gender identification. For some men and women sex, gender, and sexual orientation came together in a male or female package, but for most there were points of identification on both sides of the gender line and in real life most people cross back and forth with great fluidity. Although the dominant social order seeks to define gender roles, sexual orientation, and sociological and economic status according to anatomy, this was never true in the faith community of my youth. Men were neither from Mars nor women from Venus.

There is something very God-like about the fluidity of gender in the trans community, as God is without gender limitations but understands all of us completely. I was not surprised to learn that in the culture of Native Americans transgender people are considered the most spiritual members of their communities, unfettered by gender limitations. The whole community is reflected in them. One of my transgender parishioners once said that transgender persons are very spiritual . . . a bit like angels, not gender limited, created as a true reflection of God.

Many transgendered persons live in the Tenderloin neighborhood of San Francisco, which is also the locale of many transient hotels, drug traffic, and prostitution. It is also filled with the elderly and immigrant poor, and people with emotional disabilities. Elderly residents remain locked in their rooms, fearing to come out, as there are few safe gathering places. Runaway youth roam the streets and congregate around liquor stores. The Tenderloin (known as the "TL") is a diverse community in which people of every color and culture struggle to live and find meaning in the most depressed conditions in San Francisco. This is the neighborhood that is home to many transgendered persons and they can be seen on the streets of the Tenderloin most any time of the day or night.

Transgendered persons have suffered enormous persecution and misunderstanding from both straight and SGL people. Leslie Feinberg, a female-to-male transgender person, relates an experience where in an attempt to get a job, he borrowed a friend's wig and "feminine" clothes for the job interview. People on the bus with him pointed their fingers and whispered loud enough for Feinberg to hear, "Is that a man?" Feinberg said of the experience, "The more I tried to wear clothing or styles considered appropriate for women, the more people believed I was a man trying to pass as a woman. I began to understand that I couldn't conceal my gender expression."[27]

Transgenders do not consider themselves SGL and do not identify as such. Men who identify as women seem to have more hardships than women who identify as men, primarily because of the anatomical and external difficulty of a male body passing as female (such as facial hair and large bones). Transgendered persons are not well respected in the SGL community and are often blamed for bringing undue attention to themselves and away from the issues of the SGL community. In *States of Desire*, Edmund White maintains:

> The scorn directed against drags is especially virulent: they have become the outcasts of Gay life, the "queers" of homosexuality. In fact, they are classic scapegoats. Our old fears about sissiness, still with us though masked by the new macho fascism, are now located, isolated, and quarantined through our persecution of the transvestite.[28]

Transgender Kory Martin-Damon speaks about the devaluing of transgender persons by all communities:

> Overall, the gay, lesbian, straight, and bisexual communities devalue transsexuals because of the choices we make. When transsexuals fully transition, though for all practical purposes we are men and women, we are not always believed as the gender we present to the world. . . . As such we are somehow less than real . . . we are accepted as spectacles . . . nothing serious.[29]

The members of our transgender support group, Transcending, shared with me that most transgendered persons do not feel welcomed in any church and in very few faith communities. Churches often demonize what they do not (nor are challenged to) understand. I often reflect on the overused "God made Adam and Eve, not Adam and Steve" quote so often used in churches. I am reminded of the intersex[30] community and the total lack of understanding we have about them. How do they know which gender was God's intention? What happens if the gender chosen for them does not match what they feel oriented to be? I have intersex people in my congregation and I listen to their stories, their joys, and their struggle. They are teaching me so much about finding one's way past religion to get to God. Religious leaders know so little about human sexuality, and yet have more to say about it than any other group of people on earth.

I have met with transgendered and intersex groups enough to determine that this desire to be other-gendered is not a need to act out or show off. It is rooted in a deep sense of having been born in the wrong body, a self-awareness that is often realized at a very early age. A change in gender identification has led to enormous loss for many: loss of family, church, job/income, and health. I have counseled a number of transgendered persons who were contemplating suicide, who were victims of physical violence, and who had paid enormous sums of money for sex reassignment surgery. No one would suffer such loss simply to play games. We still have much to learn about human sexuality and how it affects psychological well-being and the possibilities of forming healthy communities.

In order to sustain community, we must not assume that we understand everyone's issues; rather, we must educate and inform each other, thereby equipping the community to receive everyone. While there are a number of transgendered persons who have gained the emotional, spiritual, and economic support to live comfortably, there remains a disproportionate number who struggle to have their basic human needs met. Our experience with many of the transgendered members of our church and the Tenderloin transgendered population has resulted in these findings: 1) Transgendered persons are or have been at great risk for substance abuse and AIDS, both due to the types of drugs used and the sharing of needles for illicit drugs such as speed and heroin. 2) Transgendered persons are often procuring hormones on the black market and are not under the supervision of a medical professional. Many transgendered persons have reported becoming ill when experimenting with a dosage or with new types of hormone therapy without the benefit of medical supervision. 3) Transgendered persons are often discriminated against in employment and, thus, turn to survival sex and crime to pay for basic living expenses, hormone therapies, and/or sexual reassignment surgery. 4) Female-to-male transgendered persons are deeply in the closet, often pass as male, and require specific care authorities as a result of prolonged use of male hormones. 5) Transgendered persons are regularly victims of violence and are discriminated against and harassed by local law enforcement agencies and by health care professionals. 6) Transgendered youth are often run out of their homes and schools and, therefore, have little choice but to engage in the sex industry and experience the myriad dangers associated with it.

The church can be made a safer place for transgendered persons by doing three things:

- Developing spiritual and practical support groups for transgendered persons within the ministry

- Providing sensitivity workshops for the congregation (all age groups)

- Involving transgendered persons in various levels of governance and decision making

Developing Spiritual and Practical Support Groups for Transgendered Persons

There is a great need for pastoral care and spiritual support for transgendered persons because this group has terrible "church burns" and a real fear of rejection and abandonment by God and people.

In the transgendered community where persons are often seeking to become fully someone else, there is often a need to obliterate all memory of a past life. This is a process that may begin and end with transdressing but may also culminate in surgical alterations and a complete change of gender identification, anatomically and legally. Support groups are structured to create an atmosphere for sharing past as well as present and future issues. This group has little desire to have their past remembered, and because much of their present is conditioned by living out the new uncharted self, it is tenuous and intrusive to seek to see transgendered persons clearly. The identity shifts violently, often for self-preservation, until the desired new self is found. Consequently, in order to make the support group safe, we cannot expect transgendered people to discuss their past lives, names, families, and other personal information unless they choose to volunteer that information. The support group should create an environment where transgendered persons are able to speak freely and candidly about their spirituality, sexual behavior, drug use, shame, self-esteem issues, and self-acceptance issues without having to be lumped with SGL and bisexual groups. A relaxed atmosphere, which engenders trust and openness, will establish patterns of greater confidentiality, mutual respect, and intimacy.

Providing Sensitivity Workshops for the Congregation (All Age Groups)

The church must exemplify the love of God to transgendered people, who are very unaccustomed to a steady and affirming presence of a loving and supportive church community. As my grandmother used to say, "Love is a 'do' word." We must demonstrate the love of God by intentionally seeking knowledge and information to better serve the transgendered community.

To this end, churches should have periodic workshops facilitated by transgendered persons that will sensitize the parishioners to the reality of the transgender life and make normative their presence in the full life of the church. Open discussions about such issues as the use of restrooms or the complexity for transgendered persons regarding whether to identify with the men's department or the women's department would give the church a better idea of how seemingly insignificant structures can harm. These workshops are particularly important for young people who identify as straight and can be very intolerant of the perceived incorrectness of the transgender reality. Meeting a real person on a one-to-one basis can do wonders for pejorative assumptions and prejudices.

Involving Transgendered Persons in Various Levels of Governance and Decision Making

Inclusion in the life of the church is as essential to transgendered persons as it is to SGL persons. Having a representative at those levels of church governance where decisions are made will empower transgendered persons. We must send the message that the church is not satisfied with a love that tolerates but desires a love that affirms and celebrates diversity. Additionally, those concerns of the transgendered members that would be otherwise overlooked may be lifted up. An atmosphere of radical inclusivity that intentionally reaches to the outer edges of society demonstrates the authentic desire of the church to sustain a community where all marginalized people can feel welcome. Whosoever will, let them come.

SAME GENDER LOVING PERSONS LIVING WITH HIV/AIDS

As a third concern I want to address the pandemic of AIDS. An ethic of compassion must be extended to those who bear the two-edged sword of being an SGL person and living with HIV/AIDS. I am aware of the presence of violent homophobia in the church world; however, SGL people have been present in the church throughout its history. This presence is creatively closeted. Certain types of constructs are very suitable for hiding in the church, particularly in monastic and convent life. In a discussion on the church and society, Episcopal Bishop John Spong said, "The priesthood in many ways is the ultimate closet in Western civilization, where gay people particularly have hidden for the past two thousand years."[31] Nevertheless, the existence of the church closet is by no means an indicator that SGL people are accepted or see themselves as acceptable. The historical position of most of the Christian church regarding homosexuality has been abundantly clear: homosexuality is an abomination, and for some religious folk, it does not matter what science or personal experience says to the contrary. Spong further states,

> Since the (scientific) evidence points to the conclusion that homosexual persons do not choose their sexual orientation, cannot change it, and constitute quite a normal but minority expression of human sexuality, it is clear that heterosexual prejudice against homosexuals must take its place alongside witchcraft, slavery, and other ignorant beliefs and oppressive institutions that we have abandoned.[32]

Unfortunately, and in spite of the scientific evidence, many SGL people have internalized the historical position of the church. Klaus Mann, son of German author Thomas Mann, revealed the frustration of his struggle with his homosexuality. He stated, "One cannot serve this Eros without becoming a stranger in society as it is today: one cannot commit oneself to this form of love without incurring a mortal wound."[33] The "fightings and fears within and without"[34] have kept many in denial. AIDS has been the great revealer; it has uncovered people who never thought their homosexual risk behavior or any other risk behavior would be fully disclosed. It has taken the doors off of many huts. According to Keith Boykin, an African American SGL man and author of *One More River to Cross: Black and Gay in America*, many prominent black leaders fear that their careers and reputations will be ruined if they are rumored to be SGL. Unless these famous, wealthy, and powerful leaders are very secure in their sexuality and careers they will avoid the topic of homosexuality and AIDS.[35] Even if they are SGL and or HIV positive, they will often avoid the subject unless they are addressing it in punitive terms. For many it is an issue of economics. Many gospel music artists who are SGL and living with AIDS will not disclose unless and until the illness exposes them. This puts them outside of clinical trials and new treatment modalities.

The reality of homophobia, homohatred, and heterosexism[36] in the church, whether internalized or externalized, has been especially oppressive to those living and dying with AIDS. AIDS is often viewed as a God-given purgative to cleanse the church of an unwelcome population, a population to which most religious organizations had no viable ministry before AIDS.

A special report prepared by the Public Media Center called *The Impact of Homophobia and Other Social Biases on AIDS* states:

> It is our contention that just as AIDS-Related Stigma is the driving force behind our nation's lackluster response to HIV/AIDS, so the unaddressed issue of homophobia remains the unseen cause of the spread of AIDS-Related Stigma within U.S. society. We believe that until the issue of homophobia is properly and adequately addressed in America, our nation is unlikely to generate an objective, focused response to the epidemic of HIV/AIDS.[37]

Homophobia kills, and not just in violence against SGL people but in the inequitable response of the church and society to the AIDS epidemic. Issues such as cigarette smoking and poor diet that lead to illness are not moralized and stigmatized in the manner that AIDS is. There have been other health threats such as Legionnaires' disease or toxic shock syndrome that received an immediate response from the media and health officials. This resulted in arresting those diseases in their genesis. I am convinced that the unwillingness of then President Reagan to mention the word AIDS until twenty thousand people were dead was due to rampant homophobia; this was nearly seven years after AIDS first appeared in the United States.

The Public Media Center report compares the response to the AIDS pandemic of most ministers to a statement from a minister during the cholera epidemic who wrote of the divine function of the illness to "promote the cause of righteousness . . . and to drain off the filth and scum which contaminate and defile human society."[38] I have heard worse from ministers and church members regarding SGL persons living with AIDS.

It is important to address the issue of being an SGL person and having AIDS because there is an insidious attempt in the church world to separate those persons who should receive compassion in the epidemic from those who should not. Those who "should" receive compassion are most often women and children, and SGL men are most often the objects of the greatest disdain. Being SGL is thought of as the supreme challenge to manhood. Author James Baldwin, an African American SGL man, defined this challenge by stating, "The condition that is now being called gay was then called queer. The operative word was faggot and later, pussy, but those epithets really had nothing to do with the question of sexual preference: You were being told simply that you had no balls."[39] These attitudes toward SGL men are systemic in American society and are at the root of homohatred. This hatred employs a god of vengeance in the form of AIDS.

Christine Smith describes the feeling of most churches toward homosexuals:

> They are judged inferior, deviant, and sick. This kind of condemnation is condoned and justified by many of our religious communities. Through its theologies, biblical interpretations, and sexual ethics, the Christian Church is one of the primary institutions that provide a foundation for social and ecclesiastical oppression of lesbians and gay men.[40]

Marriage and commitment is still well within the sphere of heterosexual privilege and not considered an option by some same-sex couples because of church-induced internalized homophobia; people who fall into this category are often involved in ongoing anonymous sexual activities to avoid being labeled as a "couple." Although some choose anonymous sex, there are the people for whom touching and being touched is limited to restrooms, rest stops, bars, bookstores, and bathhouses because they feel they have no other option. These fear-based anonymous, clandestine, and often unprotected encounters exacerbated by a constant atmosphere of abuse of all same gender loving people have contributed to the proliferation of the virus in the SGL community. The reality of virulent homohatred, heterosexism, heteronormativeness, and homophobia causes great anger and fear for gays. This fear disables potentially loving relationships, destroys self-confidence and self worth, and often leads to addictive behaviors that block out the pain of loneliness. According to Christine Smith:

> Gay and Lesbian oppression is the daily experience of being silenced when heterosexual persons may speak, being made invisible when heterosexual reality is the only reality assumed and affirmed, and being terrorized by the constant awareness that an inappropriate comment, look, reaction, or expression could change one's entire life. . . . When Lesbians and Gay men know they have a rightful place, fear is transformed.[41]

An anonymous SGL writer revealed the struggle:

> We must be prepared to tell lies to people we love and to have ready (false) answers to questions about what we've been doing, where we've been, with whom, why, and what our future plans are. Then in painful irony, we can expect to be accused of being silent and reserved, and of not sharing ourselves and our lives with our families.[42]

When SGL people are terminally ill or the significant other of someone ill they have to deal with the lack of family support and the gradual loss of friends, possessions, and future. The picture of a loving family standing around the bed of a dying loved one is most often a fantasy. The surviving partner and principal caregiver is often dismissed as someone inconsequential. In the middle of these traumatic experiences, at the point of greatest spiritual urgency, they will often attempt to reach out to a faith community for spiritual comfort. When they turn to the church, the doors are slammed shut and we have neglected a marvelous opportunity to show forth Christ, particularly when the cause for our lack of compassion is the abhorrence of people who are not heterosexual. The church and society are still places of heteroprivilege.

Ann Thompson Cook relates a series of experiences that describe heterosexual privilege:

> The person you have loved and lived with for forty years is in intensive care and you are not allowed to visit because you are not "family." During coffee breaks, your co-workers often mention their spouses or people they are dating, but you feel you must remain silent about yours. Your partner has just died of AIDS. His parents, ignoring the fact that you have been living together for ten years, are coming to sell the house you and your partner shared. You are a single, Gay man in seminary, and your married classmates in seminary are looking forward to moving into a parsonage after ordination. You wonder what will happen when you find someone you want to settle down with.[43]

LARRY THE CHRISTIAN QUEEN

The story of being SGL and living with AIDS in a heteroprivileged environment is best told by the life of Larry. Larry was an usher at our church, City of Refuge UCC. Larry could tell his story much better than I could, but a few years ago he went to sleep with the saints.

Larry (not his real name) was born into a family of African American Baptists from the South who, like so many, migrated to California during the Second World War. His mother died when he was very young, and one of his maternal aunts raised him, along with his cousins, as though he was her child. Larry attended church faithfully and participated in youth church functions.

As his early life progressed, it became evident that Larry was not a "typical" young man. After several hilarious and tragic attempts at courting women, Larry became resigned to the fact that he was same gender loving. Fortunately, his aunt pledged her support to him regardless of his sexual orientation. Unfortunately, throughout his life, her support did not—could not—shield Larry from the cruel words, gestures, innuendo, and ridicule he received from family and church members, even though he was an usher at our church. Nor could it erase the pain of Larry's separation from his father, among the most difficult experiences of Larry's life because, according to his father, it was a separation based on Larry's homosexuality.

When Larry got AIDS, many members of his family felt it was God's final word of judgment on Larry's "lifestyle" and the punishment for his disobedience. These family members used this position as the principal reason for not visiting him and leaving his care totally in the hands of the aunt who raised him. I can remember Aunt Ruth sitting by Larry's bedside like Mary the mother of Jesus, waiting for his last breath and whispering, "Boy, you know I did the best I could"—this while Larry's father walked around the room openly discussing the cost of the funeral and saying how "some young people bring these things on themselves by making the wrong decisions," all within earshot of Larry. Though Larry was one of a kind, his story contains suffering that is, unfortunately, known to many SGL people with faith.

The church and society are still places of heteroprivilege. Due to this, in response to the years of theological and spiritual abuse, some SGL people have formed spiritual communities and organizations outside of the traditional spiritual centers and oppressive environments. These communities are also recreational, sociopolitical, and empowering organizations that help to build self-esteem and provide a safe environment.

This peripheral power of newly empowered SGL persons, outside the structure of traditional religious organizations, is having a profound impact, which has lead to confrontation, engagement, and sometimes change in the concrete positions held by church prayer groups and Bible study groups. Churches are rising up. They refuse to exclude SGL persons, and fresh theology and interpretation is being born at the flash point of sexuality and spirituality.

Fellowships such as the Metropolitan Community Church, the Evangelical Network (TEN), Unity Fellowship, Reconciling Pentecostals, and Refuge Ministries have been intentional in responding to the spiritual needs of the SGL community. It is the age-old truth of a group of God's people refusing to believe that God is not a friend to them, regardless of the opinion of the dominant culture. As for Larry, he found his liberation with us in prayer, Bible study, and worship; and could he praise God! I will never forget his effervescence and expressions of joy. At his funeral we were somewhat distressed when we saw the way his father had dressed him: cheap black suit, white shirt, and dark tie—not Larryesque at all. The outfit Larry chose for his funeral was bright purple with gold buttons and tassels. Our distress was lifted when, while speaking at the funeral, one of our sister ushers commented on how she and Larry used to exchange pumps in worship service. After the laughter died down, it was clear that the man we were burying was the same one who lived so big among us as Larry the Christian Queen.

The true witness of the church requires that it be free from the stigmatization and prejudice that makes compassion and community selective and reserved for those that some in the church feel deserve it. Larry didn't necessarily get to enjoy the support our faith communities should hope to foster, but he was part of the emerging community of SGL people who have always supported the church, even if they weren't acknowledged or accepted. Let us pray that in the coming years, his is a story of the distant past and not the distant future.

SOME RECOMMENDATIONS FOR COMMUNITY LIFE

There are elements necessary to the sustenance of community that are common to all marginalized persons, two of which I refer to as voice and growth.

Voice

I have been studying the phenomenon of the twelve-step groups that rose up in the late 1930s in this country. During the course of study I began to see the similarity between the twelve-step groups and the church of my youth, the Pentecostal Church. There was a time given in the meeting when anyone who desired had an opportunity to give voice to whatever they were going through and to solicit the help and support of the group. In the Pentecostal Church it is called testimony service. In the twelve-step groups it is called sharing. Twelve-step programs and the Pentecostal Church have experienced sustained growth, and that growth is connected to the emphasis placed on giving people voice.

I have found that it is of vital importance that people who have been silent and silenced far too long be given an opportunity to give voice to their struggle. Secrets kill and silence often equals death. People often speak forth the answers to their own issues as they talk it out in a supportive environment. It also has a purgative effect on the teller of the story. Shadows are no longer threatening when the light shines on them; when the secret is exposed, the demon is uncovered and rendered powerless. The experiences that at one time horrified now become a resource from which to draw life, both for the teller and the listener. In order for a community to share in each other's failures and triumphs, occasions must be provided for testifying and sharing . . . even those things that appear obvious.

Growth

A television documentary on the growth cycle of crabs (the crustaceans) explained that crabs have an exoskeleton, or an outside skeleton, that they shed periodically. They shed the skeleton when they grow too large for it. It cracks and breaks away, and it is only during this time that the female is available to mate. Without her hard exterior, she is accessible to the male. She will reproduce in this state but she must be covered and protected because she is extremely vulnerable.

Marginalized, bruised, and wounded people grow in much the same way. I said earlier that there is a period of cathartic vulnerability when marginalized people initially feel accepted in a Christian community. This vulnerability lasts until the person feels stronger and more confident. It is as dangerous to be constantly vulnerable and cathartic as it is to have a false sense of invulnerability. In the growth cycle, when the old shell is shed a new shell begins to grow that both protects some things from getting out and other things from getting in. It guards the emotions to allow time for reflection and introspection. It protects until the next level of challenge exposes areas of weakness and then new growth takes place; then one has to break out again . . . and be vulnerable. Vulnerability and weakness often result in growth, but the one growing must be covered and protected during this season. This is also the best time to reproduce or draw others. At the point of greatest vulnerability, we are most accessible, compassionate, and interdependent on each other and dependent on God. Sustaining community requires an understanding of the ebb and flow of the growth cycle and the provision of a safe place to go through the cycles.

The Christian community on the margin will concretize into a force when it has intimacy and experience with God and defines and sustains healthy boundaries, while making room for growth and change. Before celebration can occur, however, the community must look closely at how it perceives itself. What is the location of the celebration, when so many people have so many issues in the process of being addressed, healed, relieved, and resolved? I assert that the community cannot truly celebrate itself until individuals begin to "see" themselves and each other through the eyes of faith . . . the eyes of God.

CELEBRATING COMMUNITY

From now on, therefore, we regard no one from a human point of view; even though we once knew Christ from a human point of view, we know him no longer in that way. So if anyone is in Christ, there is a new creation: everything old has passed away; see, everything has become new! All this is from God, who reconciled us to himself through Christ, and has given us the ministry of reconciliation; that is, in Christ God was reconciling the world to himself, not counting their trespasses against them, and entrusting the message of reconciliation to us. So we are ambassadors for Christ, since God is making his appeal through us; we entreat you on behalf of Christ, be reconciled to God. For our sake he made him to be sin who knew no sin, so that in him we might become the righteousness of God. (2 Cor. 5:16–20)

SEEING CLEARLY

IN *The Tyranny of Beauty*, Arline and John Liggett explore the history of dangerous procedures women have undergone in the quest for beauty. They claim that most of these things were done so that women could be desired by men, thus improving their economic status.[1] I was amazed at how women, over the centuries, have mauled and manipulated just about every body part—lips, eyes, ears, waists, skulls, foreheads, and feet. As the idea of beauty changed, we would shift, stretch, and manipulate our bodies to fit a particular era's cookie-cutter fashion and to survive economically in male-dominated societies. In our time of breast implants, Botox, anorexia, and liposuction we often fail to recall that this is nothing new.

In China, girls had their feet bound, crippling them for life, but ensuring the three- or four-inch-long "lotus blossom foot" prized as feminine. The foot would be folded in half until the blood supply was cut off to a major portion, which would subsequently rot and fall away.

In central Africa, the Mangbettu wrapped the heads of female infants to attain the elongated cone-shaped heads considered a sign of intelligence and beauty, but which in fact caused permanent brain damage.

In Queen Victoria's England, snow white, porcelain-like skin was achieved with a paste called ceruse that contained lead and eventually ate away at the skin, leaving deep holes.

And then there was the perplexingly long-lived corset. At times in history it was designed to be worn so tightly that women tended to faint, unable to breathe deeply enough to get sufficient oxygen to their brains.

In *Neanderthal*, John Darnton talks about a people of a simpler time.[2] In this fictional tale, Darnton tries to explain why there have been so many historical sightings of a hominid—larger than us, very hirsute, and extremely muscular, but not ever taken into captivity. Darnton hypothesizes that this hominid is the Neanderthal man who had the ability to communicate telepathically as opposed to communicating by language or speech. This hypothesis explains the sightings of the yeti, the abominable snowman, and bigfoot. According to the story, these creatures had no crime, no struggle for power or control; no one among them could misrepresent themselves because everyone knew the truth. They could not hide from each other, but humans seldom saw them. They could sense when we humans were around and, by experience, knew that the two-legged hairless ones could not be trusted. The author is implying that when we connect with someone by spoken language alone, we can easily deceive. This author surmises that homo sapiens won over Neanderthal by learning a language and therefore learning to lie, cheat, and deceive.

What do these messages tell us about our humanity? First, we see to what extent some have altered their bodies for survival and others for conceit. Second, we see how deceitful external communication and appearance can be. Although the story is fiction, what a great joy it would be to know and be known in the limitless realm of the spirit, with no further need to pretend to be someone we are not. There is an African proverb that says, "I am not my present reality; I am my truth."

Paul begins the teaching in 2 Corinthians 5:16 with a strong injunction: "From now on, therefore, we regard no one from a human point of view even though we once knew Christ from a human point of view." If we had known of Jesus in his time on earth we probably would not have thought much of him, as he was born in a little obscure town in rebellious Galilee to a teenage mother, under dubious circumstances. He was an unemployed laborer, a tradesman, who never married and led a band of followers who were constantly eating at other people's houses. Jesus was deemed subversive by the religious and political powers of his day. He was arrested, tried, condemned to die, and executed. That was his reality. His truth was that he held in his bosom the power of resurrection . . . the ability to bring life out of death. If we did not know the truth of Jesus according to the Spirit and by faith, what would we really think of him?

We must prioritize knowing each other deeper than what our eyes can see because celebrating community that is truly diverse requires a new way of seeing and a new way of being.

The Scripture passage implies that we can celebrate one another in some new and powerful way in Christian community—some way that both accepts who each of us is in a human sense and transcends our humanity, allowing us to see each other as God sees us.

"Now you know each other according to the spirit. All things have changed." We have become a new creation, something unprecedented. We move in a different sphere and we have been given a new task. We have a new covenant. We have a new ministry. It is the ministry of reconciliation.

We must acknowledge, see, and know people by more than externals for a celebration of community authentically to take place. People who are marginalized expose a great deal, but if we are basing all that is known on what is exposed to us, we have still missed the boat. As I have said earlier, simply seeing someone's issues does not create, sustain, or give cause to celebrate community. We may see who we are with our eyes but we can only see what we shall become by faith. Reconciliation and communion with God or each other cannot take place where relationship is only skin deep and does not discern the gift of God in each of us. The connecting point is much deeper than the obvious.

Many relationships are not long lived—not because anyone is at fault, but because at the point of real contact, where spirit meets spirit, the true person emerges and is quite different than our first impression. Often this true person is not at all the person we thought they were and we are either disappointed or pleasantly surprised. When we attend deeply to the persons in our surroundings, we begin to see them according to the Spirit. We begin to behold or perceive more than the external. We cannot help each other become reconciled to God if we see only the outward presentation. We must look deeper. What is really there, even in the one we struggle with, the one with the most complex personality? Christian community can truly be celebrated when we realize the church is a spiritual, mystical, faith-based community, and we relate best when we make the drop from head to heart.

PREACHING TO COMMUNITY[1]

I AM A DESPERATE PREACHER who knows personally how theologies are fluid and new ones are born at friction points. My voice is rooted in the African American Southern Pentecostal Church, where passion for God in Jesus is heard and seen in the songs, preaching, dancing, and daily at-home meditations. I have struggled with the history of the church and the interpretation of the Bible, but not with the freestyle celebratory worship of the Pentecostal Church. My struggle has been with the Christian church's changing position regarding the treatment of women, same gender loving persons, war, people of color, and slaves. (My grandmother, Bessie Hamilton, born in 1895, was the daughter of Stella Wyatt, who was born a slave.) I am an avowed womanist and a reconciling liberation theologian who dances in the Spirit and speaks in tongues. Holding on to Jesus in spite of the church and the tortured interpretations of scripture, which used to mortally wound my people and my faith, has been a lifelong journey. Finding my way, following the Light, refusing to believe Jesus didn't love me/us; this is the foundation of my preaching.

Mine is a voice that passionately preaches justice and freedom with responsibility, however, not to the exclusion of Jesus. Justice without Jesus will not work for me.

I preach to a desperate people, who are struggling to make sense of their lives on the margins of society. They are my beloveds.

In my community, you must find God in the struggle for equality, parity, and justice; the struggle is the long, strong, deep, resonant base of all I preach, sing, and pray about. "Through many dangers, toils, and snares" is foundational to our worship, and the locus of our passion. If we cannot see God in the struggle and believe day after day that God will make it all right, then we cannot see God at all. This is the starting point.

I preach faith-based sermons to build self-worth and self-value in the lives of people who have often been stripped of all that is right and good. I strive to see peace and a sense of security present in the lives of those I pastor, preach to, and serve. Emil Thomas said that "our slave ancestors had a basis for calm: a special inner peace born of a profound conviction that their self-worth had been well established already and was guaranteed by the Ruler of the universe."[2] This is a peace born from the assurance that God will come through for us; God is on our side. This is what I believe; this is what I preach.

PREACHING INFLUENCES

I identify with Craddock in his book *Preaching* because his approach to preaching/teaching is very Bible, Jesus, and God centered.[3] I've seen the methods he recommends for sermon structure used both in the United Church of Christ, where I serve at present, and in the churches of my youth; however, what flows out of his center is scripture-based preaching with other sources used to support the scripture. While I am not in total agreement with the extent to which Craddock lifts up the authority of the Bible, I do appreciate and believe strongly in scripture-based, Christ-centered preaching for liberation. This kind of preaching requires study with an eye to taking Jesus back from the fundamentalists, but it is the most effective kind of preaching for my community. I, like David Buttrick, would argue "for a church animated by the Gospel, rather than a church heavily under the rule of an imposed scriptural authority,"[4] but people who have for generations been abused by the preaching of the Bible need to hear the Bible preached in ways that affirm and validate them.

Preaching in my tradition uses life experience, or what I call "personal transparency" to identify with the experiences of the listener.

There is a need for the preacher to be sensitive to the needs of the listener—that is, sermons should speak for as well as to the congregation; the gospel is from the community as well as to it. There is also a need for honesty and intimacy, and it is important to preach using themes, hymns, and stories that are familiar to the listener.

I believe that in order to genuinely be a blessing to the congregation the preacher must seek to know and understand to whom she/he is preaching. Lenora Tubbs Tisdale in *Preaching as Local Theology and Folk Art* calls this "exegeting the congregation." Tisdale says,

> If we as preachers are going to proclaim the Gospel in ways capable of transforming congregational identity, we first need to become better acquainted with the ways our people already imagine God and the world. If we are going to aid in the extension of myopic vision or the correction of astigmatic values then we must first strive to "see" God and the world as our people do.[5]

It is through this synergistic relationship that the preacher and the congregation become one organism, worshiping God together. The preaching and the response are then filled with faith, passion, and power. This is preaching, as I understand it. New and difficult truths should be packaged in a familiar wrapping, so a common relationship of trust based on collective experience can be established. Preaching that is outside of the theological, intellectual, or cultural reach of the listener is an insult to the life experience the listener brings to the preaching moment. It is not enough for me to simply be profound but I seek to be a profound blessing, by hearing from God and paying close attention to the "voice" of the listening congregation.

My preaching is greatly influenced by my grandfather, my stepfather, my uncles, my mother, and my grandmother, all of whom are or were preachers. I spent my youth as a pastor's kid in the Church of God in Christ, a predominately black Pentecostal denomination. My style of preaching echoes the preachers who surrounded me, both in my family and throughout the organization. Most of the preachers I knew were blue-collar folk who came to their role as preacher and/or pastor without the benefit of formal training. There were not many African

Americans in college, and if they were in school they were seeking a way to make themselves more eligible for jobs.

The call to preach was not often planned as a vocation. It sort of ran up behind you and tackled you while you were trying to get ahead in life. Authorization for ministry came from the church at such time as it was determined one was ready. "Ready" meant having demonstrated faithfulness and an ability to preach. The Church of God in Christ believed that no matter how educated or filled with deep knowledge a person was, that knowledge had to be evidenced by good preaching for a preacher to gain affirmation from the church. Good preaching meant good performance that included choosing a good text, a good reading of the text, good entertainment, believability/authority, identification, food for thought, power, humor, passion, and a super celebration. I know that Craddock's statement "Listeners tend to lean into narratives which have emotional force, but which are presented with emotional restraint"[6] is an indication that we come from different cultures. Emotional restraint was not exercised particularly at the close or celebration time in the sermon.

I tend to agree with Frank A. Thomas regarding celebration and emotion. Thomas writes, "It is precisely because so much of Western preaching has ignored emotional context and process, and focused on cerebral process and words, that homileticians most recently have struggled for new methods to effectively communicate the Gospel."[7] The preaching was central to the worship experience; it was the highlight. All things lead up to it and out from it. It was a Word from God.

I am fascinated when I read books like *Speaking from the Heart* that detail the performance model often present in black Pentecostal preaching and lift up that method as an example of how good preaching is accomplished.[8] I find myself often wishing that my Grandpa Eugene (Bishop Eugene E. Hamilton) and my Uncle Rudolph (Bishop S. Rudolph Martin) could have lived long enough for me to share with them the fact that a science is being taught that captures what they did among us for many years. They did not adhere to any particular preaching calendar or use many sermon helps written by others, but the power of their sermons lives on.

Of particular interest is the "science" and skill I now recognize in the preaching I grew up around; I know most of those folk did not realize what masters they were in the art of using illustrations, simile, or hyperbole, but all these things were part of their preaching process and, by inheritance, part of mine.

Storytelling, speaking in hieroglyphics, and using word pictures were methods employed to leave a lasting impression on the hearer. You could see it, taste it, and feel it while they preached. My grandpa lived his sermons so his ethos and personal conviction came through with great passion, energy, and emotion.

The Pentecostal preaching influence is one where the language is ordered, the lines are metrical and poetic, and the sermon is "sung" in places with the help of the congregation and the musicians. This form of performance art entertained the congregation while driving home the truths in the sermon. Engaging the audience in a call and response to both the meter and the message not only encouraged the congregation to participate but it signaled that the sermon was successful. Preaching as performance art was and is an essential part of the African American Pentecostal worship experience.

HOW I COME TO THE PREACHING MOMENT

Reading is a passion for me. I read history, literature, scripture, magazines, web articles, newspapers, and anything else I can get my hands on. In my reading I listen for themes of freedom with responsibility, hope, perseverance, culture, and real people. I look deeply into the characters in scripture for their humanity and how they identify with us. I want to demystify the saints while not losing respect for their struggle. I seek to know by revelation and through literature contemporary with the text what things the writers and interpreters did not tell us. We all keep secrets, so what would they rather we did not know? What is it they assumed we would understand? What meanings have been lost or changed with time? What is the truth under the writings? I seek to bring those things to the preaching moment.

INCARNATIONAL INTERPRETATION

I seek for a fresh method to interpret scripture, for I know there must be a new, more faithful way to handle the text that can move me to a method that faithfully embodies the feelings, message, and spirit of the original creator. I would go further and suggest that it is the faithful embodiment of the text and the writer that enables incarnational preaching. It is a work of the Holy Spirit. With all of our study and faithful attention to the text, we struggle with seeing what is truly there, because what we see is often not what is there. What we see, what we read is often what the text has come to mean synthesized through lenses fashioned for our place in time. The Holy Spirit must help us grasp the original form and melt into it. The spirit in the interpreter and the spirit in the originator must connect spirit to spirit, heart to heart, sometimes over centuries in a long-distance love relationship. It would seem that this would be extremely difficult unless there were some mutual and similar experience between the interpreter and the character being embodied. I see and feel real people in the scripture who had struggles not unlike mine.

In the history of black music there was a type of music referred to as Negro spirituals. These songs, filled with eschatological metaphors, could be taken at face value for the original art form that they are. The words could be embraced and the appropriate interpreter could embody the form or the experience of the slave authors and sing with passion of the hope and the dream of the slave—"Soon Ah Will Be Don wid de Trubbles ob de Worl" or "Swing Low Sweet Chariot" or "Saint Peter Open Dem Gates." However, if that someone did not know the code in the language of the songs and relate to the necessity of the oppressed to create a form of communication not understood by the oppressor, they might well come away having faithfully and lovingly connected to an assumption. Years and years of lacquering over both the text and our perceptions of it beg the question, is seeing believing? I think not in many cases, and we can only connect spirit to spirit.

Additionally, through lens of culture and time, the vision of the originator of the poem, song, or text may have been quite different from that of the interpreter. I am reminded of a cartoon I once saw that described how people excavating in our country five thousand years in the future might interpret our domiciles. The beautiful porcelain work of art created by someone named "Toilet" was of particular note. Can the translated and revised language faithfully communicate the values, stance, posture, and physical attitude intended by the originator without some analysis of the originator and her/his environment and culture and some work of the Spirit? Essentially the meaning of words and all artistic expressions are relative to the culture they proceed from. When the text says tree, is it the tree I relate to that I envision, or is there something totally different that would never enter my mind as tree, but the meaning of which would drastically change my understanding of the text?

I love the scripture and I constantly seek a faithful, loving way to hold and embody the text, informed by the Holy Spirit, with an eye to the culture and the changes in perception that speak to how the text comes to us.

I never know what I am going to preach from one Sunday to the next. The sermon subject matter comes through a song I hear, or a scripture or a book I read, or an experience I share with someone . . . some word or principle comes to my attention and my spirit says, "ah-ha, that will preach." I tend to write the thought down on anything that I can find, because I know it is preaching fodder. I experience great joy when a fresh Word comes to me for my people, because I know God is communicating with my spirit. I often don't do anything with the thought for a time; I just let it sit and simmer in my spirit, while I think and pray about the scriptural and human context for the sermon.

There are often two or three sermon pots simmering simultaneously, and the last one may be first and the first one may be last. Other things come to witness to the truth that has already been deposited in me. The scriptures, examples, parables, and stories that bring the thought to life come in waves, when I am bathing or driving or working on something else. I keep something handy to write with all the time. I have little notes everywhere that I accumulate when I come to my computer to pull the sermon together.

When the sermon is ready to be preached it is always brief on paper, because I know I will get the rest of it in the pulpit. I need the people and the Holy Spirit working in the preaching moment to finish the sermon. I have often taken the same notes with me to different occasions, and preached totally different sermons each time.

PREACHING ON THE EDGE

As to the content of my sermons, I often preach sermons to raise the consciousness of those who feel they have exclusive rights to Jesus and to empower oppressed people to take their place at God's welcome table. I preach to build faith and to demystify success for oppressed people. I do not consider my preaching adversarial or divisive. As I mentioned earlier I call myself a reconciling, liberation theologian, and my desire is to see harmony in the body of Christ.

Empowerment and liberation are consistent themes in my preaching. Marginalized people often ask, "Is God for us?" Incarnational liberating preaching is vital in these communities, as preaching has often been used to push oppressed people more and more to the margin. The preaching in the community evidences the extent to which the community is welcoming. After a natural disaster, people come to church in record numbers asking, "Is God for us?" and then they listen for the assurance from the pulpit. In marginalized communities, crisis is a way of life and incarnational preaching is essential.

Preaching to people who are on the edge of society and the mainline church must have good content and good form. Preaching to marginalized people must be believable, powerful, and passionate. Marginalized people frequently remember strong words from the pulpit used to destroy. They need stronger words of affirmation and inclusion. In my sermons I attempt to carry a message that counters the teaching of those who support a theology that calls anyone unclean or claims to have exclusive "truth."

TOWARD A TRANSFORMING MOMENT

I believe there must be a relationship between loving and knowing God, the text, and the people the text is shared with. When the interpreter of the text begins by incorporating integrity, relatedness, and faithfulness to a relationship with God and to the text there will be a more honest relationship to the congregation/listeners. Additionally preachers must be secure in their relationship with God and witnesses of the truth of the gospel. Oppressed people seem to be particularly aware when there is disparity between what the preacher says and what she/he really believes. Ward asserts, "If you do not have a secure sense of self and conviction about your right to address your people, then it will be nearly impossible to engage them."[9]

Marginalized people are people that need to hear from God. How can they hear without a preacher? And the preacher must love God, love the text, and identify with the people in order to be authentic.

When these things come together I believe we achieve the moment of transformation. I seek for this moment in my preaching. I have no greater joy than to embody a liberating truth and to participate in the circle dance as the Holy Spirit brings life to me and to those that hear and receive the Word. God in Christ through the Holy Spirit is empowering the preacher and the congregation through the embodied Word. The circle is complete, and the kingdom is revealed. It is a glimpse of heaven.

PART TWO

Sermons

MANAGING THE THORN

2 Corinthians 12:1–10

THE THORN

"A thorn was given me in the flesh, a messenger of Satan to torment me" (2 Cor. 12:7b). Paul had a problem. It was something that brought him great sorrow and perpetual embarrassment. It was connected to how he was perceived by people. It probably caused people to say, "Look at him. He talks faith and power, so why can't he free himself from this thing? Why doesn't his Jesus deliver him? It must be something he is doing wrong." It made him look weak when he came to the churches physically. It made him the brunt of jokes and some rejoiced at the suffering because they despised Paul's gift. It often caused him to defend himself by lifting up the work he had done and the miracles wrought through his ministry (2 Cor. 11). We are inclined to defend ourselves constantly when we feel misunderstood.

What ever it was, it was a constant irritation that kept his attention and threatened to distract him from the work of ministry. He had constant thoughts and prayers about how much better off he would be without the thorn, how much stronger he would seem and how much more respected he would be. Apparently Paul believed that prayer would move this thing, perhaps because he had seen such deliverance come to others he prayed for. Paul sought God in private—probably embarrassed to tell others what he was seeking deliverance from. Why could he not get free?

What was the source of this thing, this thorn? This aggravation was prescribed by God and was, according to Paul, administered by Satan. All that Satan does to us must be with permission, which indicates the final outcome (Isa. 54:16–17). It was God's gift to Paul. God used Satan to stop Satan's own plan for Paul. What was Satan's plan? Same as it is for us. To use the thorn to distract, discourage, depress, and eventually stop Paul's effectiveness and ministry. Satan always believes evil can defeat God's purpose. I think that is part of Satan's curse, the delusion that we will be destroyed by the power of suffering. Satan doesn't seem to know how suffering empowers us. Never feel envious of anyone's abundant spiritual gift as God of necessity attaches a messenger of Satan, an errand imp with a designer thorn to keep pride in check.

The purpose was to teach spiritual dependence and community interdependence. Liberty is one thing, independence is quite another. To be liberated is to be free from the restrictions wrongfully placed on us by another. To be independent is to be free from every tie and dependent on nothing and no person—that is also a delusion and a fallacy. To be interdependent is to acknowledge the importance of doing one's part, but it also acknowledges the need for something or someone outside of one's self. We are all dependent on something or someone in some way—possibly the doctor or the plumber who knows things we don't know and upon whose skill we must depend. And if nothing else, we are dependent on God, for in God we live, move, and have our being. All of us ought to be free but none of us ought to even seek to be independent. The spirit of independence is a spirit of pride.

The potential for Paul's pride was located in his gifts and revelations. Even before he came to know Christ he was a formidable man, skilled in the law and languages . . . probably an overachiever to compensate for his self-perceived weakness. But on the road to Damascus while seeking to demonstrate the extent of his commitment to the law, his culture, and his God, Paul met Jesus in a great spiritual experience. After he came to know Christ he continued to experience powerful revelations and was given great gifts for the purpose of his calling. He was to go to the Gentiles and expand the boundaries of the faith to include those who were thought of as unclean.

A new and living way was coming alive in Paul's spirit and he had great insight and vision. He was the man who was called to write most of what came to be called the New Testament and his life journey would affect believers for generations to come. With all of this Paul had to be tempered and balanced or he had the potential to spin out of control . . . to float away full of pride like a hot air balloon without sandbags. Spiritual pride is the worst kind. And if Paul, as pious and deep as he was, needed a thorn, how about us?

God intended the thorn, not as a stumbling block or a hindrance, but rather as a catalyst for Paul's power and authority. God cannot truly use us until we are consciously weak before God . . . until there is no shadow of doubt who is in control . . . until we get out of competition with God for God's glory. It was important that Paul understand what rejection felt like if he was to effectively minister to the rejected, and he could not do the work of ministry in Asia Minor while constantly boasting of his education, citizenship, and experience in "Third Heaven." God set this pious Pharisee up by first allowing him to be ill received by the brethren because he persecuted the saints, then subjecting him to the thorn.

The thorn led Paul to earnest prayer—the kind of pouring out of the soul that goes beyond pretense. What would turn us to this kind of prayer but a thorn? And Paul kept calling until God responded.

We have great gifts. We are designers, poets, singers, musicians, health professionals, lawyers, clinician computer whizzes, etc. So much collective wisdom and ability and so many thorns. So what is keeping us from turning the world upside-down for Christ? What hinders us from sharing this great gift of knowing intimacy with God in Christ? We fear the thorn. The thorn says, "Don't get too far out there . . . don't let your relationship with God go public or I will come out and embarrass you and put you to shame. Keep your dreams and expectations minimal and small; maybe the real issues won't be noticed. Don't be too transparent or you'll be exposed."

Where we have missed our victory is in allowing the thing—the thorn—to constantly defeat our forward mobility. We feel that because we hate it and it is a messenger of Satan, then God must hate us when we are not free from it. So why won't God set us free? God can, but won't.

The thorn has moved from being a tool for our growth and is disguising itself as an instrument for our defeat and an object of perpetual distraction. It is time to overcome it.

THE PROMISE

"My Grace is sufficient for you, for power is made perfect in weakness" (2 Cor. 12:9a). Grace is God's favor; not given to us by our merit . . . we could not earn it. Grace is the heart of God extended to us and the power of God made available to us. Grace makes us able to be what God commands us to be. Grace both ensures our victory at the end of the journey and walks with us day by day. Grace cancels out sin's power and penalty in our lives.

Grace, *charis*, is opposite of *hamartia*, or sin. We cannot be both under sin and under grace (Rom. 5:1–2). Grace cancels out the power of sin and brings us into close fellowship with God through Christ, where we have access to all spiritual gifts in Christ. Grace enables us to press toward God's standard for our lives and then makes up the difference when we miss the mark both here and in eternity. Grace will make it all come together and work together for good. Grace takes the chance out of our eternity with Christ. God's unmerited favor and pardon will carry us through no matter what our weaknesses are. We are justified by faith and kept by grace. The gifts that come with justification and salvation have no relation to human merit; they are eternal and are wrought by God. What are some of these grace gifts that God gives us because of Christ's sacrifice?

> We are the elect of God and precious.
> We are the chosen.
> We are the called.
> We are redeemed.
> We are reconciled.
> We are forgiven.
> We are free from the law.
> We are the children of God.
> We are regenerated.

We are born again.

We are adopted.

We are made acceptable to God.

We are made righteous.

We are positionally sanctified (holy).

We are perfected forever.

We are justified.

We are delivered from the power of darkness.

We are translated to the kingdom of Christ.

We are a gift from God to Christ.

We are inducted into the royal priesthood, chosen generation, and holy nation.

We are citizens of heaven.

We share in Christ's inheritance.

We have the Holy Spirit as our guide and seal.

We are complete in Christ.

What need have we to have the burden removed if God will give us the sufficient grace to bear it? What does the weight of the burden matter if there is equal strength to bear it? Why be pulled from the fire designed to make us better servants before we are refined, if God will give us the requisite grace to endure?

God's grace is sufficient for what?

Our labor, which often discourages us;

Our struggles, which often frighten us;

Our suffering, which often depresses us.

We can depend on the grace of God to be sufficient to make us glory in our tribulation, because we are assured of God's presence and power. Why shrink back from our call because of our weakness when God's power is made perfect in it? This eliminates using the thorn as an excuse to neglect our call and destiny. The promise of sufficient grace is a joy not to those who sit and moan about the thorn but to those who go on in spite of it.

Depending on God's grace brings us into unity with ourselves; it integrates us and helps us to give our difficult processes time. Grace expands the narrowness of religion by setting us free from fear of divine retribution and giving us room and time to grow into the full will of God for our lives. Knowing we have God's favor changes our hearts and minds and lives.

Grace gives the poor wondrous patience and trust.

Grace makes the sick man or woman more concerned about ministering to the visitor than complaining about the sickness.

Grace woos the angry violent man and calms the beast within.

Grace loves the hell out of us.

Grace holds us like a womb . . . connected and safe while we grow.

We can go though the valley of the shadow of death by the grace of God. It is sufficient for whatever we must face. Extraordinary grace comes with extraordinary challenges and will not manifest until you are in the struggle. It is easy to believe in past grace and hope for future grace, but trusting that God is holding us up in the middle of the mess is a true challenge to our faith. But know this . . .

Grace is unlimited.

Grace is unmerited—you cannot earn it, and it is a gift that comes with Christ's purchase of us at Calvary.

Grace is making your trouble useful to you and making you triumphant over it.

Grace is prepared to bring you out of a thousand more difficulties just like this one, until you see Jesus face to face.

Grace is sufficient to avert whatever would harm you.

Grace is ready to supply whatever is good for you.

This wonderful power can only be revealed and clearly seen when we are in trouble. How else would we know we can be kept through anything until we go through something? No test, no testimony. God's strength is made perfect or at its highest potential when we are weakest. You see grace at work when Jesus said, "Forgive them, for they know not what they do." Look at the people Jesus chose to work through. A Gentile doctor, some fishermen, a tax collector, a harlot . . . I am sure that the ultrareligious voices of Jesus' time on earth said that Jesus' ministry would not last six months, but Jesus and his folks and the many who followed them turned the world upside down. Look at us. God can and will use people who know they need a savior. We do our greatest singing, our greatest preaching, our greatest writing, and our greatest giving when we are weakest.

You may read about the grace of God in the Bible or in books. You may hear about it in a sermon but you don't know about it until you are in desperate need of a savior and God comes through. When our weakness is thoroughly felt, then the strength of God can be made perfect in us. The strength of God is not perfected until our weakness is perfected. That's where some of us are now, in the process of having our weakness perfected. Our stuff that has been buried and squashed is coming up and out. It is oozing out of hidden places and folk are seeing who we really are. We are leaking. Now that we see it, it won't help to get mad, or depressed, or to cover or to blame . . . maybe it is time to surrender the weakness into the hands of the only one who loves us in spite of everything and see what Jesus intends to do with the rest of our lives.

THE RESOLVE

"So, I will boast all the more gladly of my weaknesses, so that the power of Christ may dwell in me. Therefore I am content with weaknesses, insults, hardships, persecutions, and calamities for the sake of Christ; for whenever I am weak, then I am strong" (2 Cor. 12:9b–10).

Paul had tried desperately to succeed at being a righteous man and felt he had failed miserably. He still could not make the war in his flesh nor his thorn go away (Rom. 7). He suffered until he received the revelation of faith, grace, and power . . . reoccurring themes in his writing. *Faith* as the path to salvation, not good works and rituals; *grace* or God's unmerited favor, unending love, concern, and enablement; and *power* from Christ to both will and do after God's good pleasure. Paul saw the end of the journey, so he was able to put the present squarely in the hands of Jesus.

Paul had earnestly desired the thorn to be removed and now just as earnestly he desires to let it remain, rejoice in it, and leave it to God's grace. Paul received a completely new view of life. He learned a new lifestyle—how to manage his thorn and not be managed by it was the source of attaining the power of Christ. Paul wanted the power of Christ to rest or dwell on him, not touch him and go.

Paul came to understand what true power is. We are tempted to admire and to yearn for power based on human definition. Great conquerors and rulers get human attention. King Saul of old got the people's attention. He was strong, he was tall, he was handsome, and he was a great warrior. David got God's attention. He was a shepherd, he was small, he was young, and he was weak by human standards . . . what was the difference? Saul trusted in himself and witches, David trusted in God. God was his shepherd, and God made him greater than all of his adversaries. Even when he failed God, God still called him a man after God's own heart.

Who but God can turn a curse into a blessing, making the very thing that used to bring such sorrow now a source of greatest joy?

Christ was called gluttonous, a winebibber, and a devil; yet he kept his eye on his purpose, not on the slander. He did not adjust or change anything in his plan based on what the slanderers said about him. Christ is now the one friend that slander cannot alienate; nothing said about us will drive Jesus from us (Rom. 8:38–39).

Paul gloried in the thorn. We can glory in the thorn because it makes us tender toward those who also suffer. We can encourage them to look to God so their suffering will have value. Since we all must suffer, our suffering should be for something. What greater value is there than to have the power of Christ rest upon us?

We can glory in our weakness because while we are weak in one way we are receiving supernatural strength in another. Just as the blind person excels in hearing and touch, the area where God wants us to excel is greatly enhanced by our weakness in another area. When God gets a hold on our weakness it becomes another thing and works under another law. Our weakness is transfigured into strength. God not only helps us with our weaknesses but also transforms them into power.

Paul wanted the power of Christ to dwell, rest, or tabernacle with him. Just like the *Shekinah* power dwelt in the tent in the wilderness—the Shekinah, or the visible and manifest presence of God's power and glory—a cloud rested over the mercy seat (or ark lid) between the cherubim atop the Ark of the Covenant. What was the ark? It was a simple box of wood overlaid with gold. What was its significance? It was what rested upon it. The Shekinah power of God's presence rested upon the ark and God's glory made it holy. Paul was offering his weak and frail self as a habitation or a resting-place for Christ's abiding presence and power. He was making his internal storage empty and available to Christ. He was saying to Christ, "Rest on me; take up your abode in me. I don't want my need for glory and attention to stand in the way of your glory. Let me pass out of sight behind you. Take center stage, Jesus. Glorify yourself through me!

> I am just the lamp; you are the light! Shine, Jesus, shine!
> I am the dancer; you've got the moves! Dance, Jesus, dance!
> I am the instrument; you are the melody! Sing, Jesus, sing!
> And I am just the temple; you are the Presence. Show yourself
> strong in me, Jesus, for your own glory! Amen!

SOMEONE HAS STOLEN JESUS

John 20:10–15

THEN THE DISCIPLES RETURNED to their homes. But Mary stood weeping outside the tomb. As she wept, she bent over to look into the tomb and she saw two angels in white, sitting where the body of Jesus had been lying, one at the head and the other at the feet.

They said to her, "Woman, why are you weeping?"

She said to then, "They have taken away my Lord, and I do not know where they have laid him." When she had said this, she turned around and saw Jesus standing there, but she did not know that it was Jesus.

Jesus said to her, "Woman why are you weeping? Whom are you are looking for?"

Supposing him to be the gardener, she said to him, "Sir, if you have carried him away, tell me where you have laid him, and I will take him away."

"You see, he died day before yesterday . . .

"We placed him in a snug comfortable tomb, secure from the elements and external influences. We put him where we could find him. All of his miracles are behind him, you see. He's dead . . . and death is the end. All he could do he has done already. I loved him. I served him. I am here to maintain him. I did not come here for an event, as there will be no more crowds. I came to be alone one last time with my Jesus."

This woman was in deep grief and loss. Her future hopes were dashed, her senses callused. She was worn out from the events of the last two days. She had witnessed the most horrific events of her life and experience. Jesus had been taken and brutally beaten, wrongfully judged, mockingly tried, and horribly crucified. Why hadn't heaven intervened? She'd kept looking to the sky for the avenging angels . . . looking to the horizon for the legions of God's army to rush in and set him free. How could this be? He was not ordinary! Yet they broke him.

They killed him. They took him and put him in this cold tomb . . . she saw it for herself . . . and now Jesus was not where he was supposed to be. Jesus was not only dead but also missing. She knew they hated him. What might they be doing to the precious body of the one she loved so much? She came looking for her Jesus and wherever they had taken him, she was willing to go get him, pick him up, and carry him back to his tomb. You see, a form of Jesus, a shell of Jesus is better than no Jesus at all. At least she could look at the shape of his lips that spoke softly to her, the curve of his hands that touched and healed her, and she could remember . . .

She went to find the remains of her Jesus to care for him as he had cared for her. She knew that the way it had been was over. She remembered he had been pulled from the garden and taken from judge to judge, handled by hateful hands and discarded as just another expendable religious fanatic.

And she loved him, though she did not really know who he was— or now, where he was. And on this morning of all mornings she needed him to at least be where he was supposed to be.

It is great grief to those who believe they know Jesus, when the Jesus they know is taken away, or is transformed from the Jesus they were accustomed to. This is seldom thought of as a time to rejoice.

Where was he? Who took him, and how could she get him back? Could it be that her need to find Jesus where she left him hindered her from seeing where he was?

Can our need to keep Jesus where we need him blind us to where Jesus is moving today?

Can it be that our need to hear Jesus say what we believe he has always said, keeps us from hearing what he is saying today?

Can our need to confine Jesus keep us from participating in the real power of his resurrection? Do we waste our time by looking in a graveyard for a living, dancing, glorified Jesus?

Now let's not think little of Mary. She represents many who are loyal, vigilant, and faithful to attending a graveyard where Jesus used to be and asking, "Where have they taken him? Where is the Jesus I know?"

"Where did you take him?" she asked.

Someone said, "We've got him. He's over here!"

"He now dwells behind stained glass and in the vaulted ceilings of mighty gothic cathedrals. He flies in buttresses. He resides in shrines and holy places . . . in relics and shrouds.

"He whispers a lot."

"No, we've got him!" said another.

"Jesus is walking among things political and national. Jesus is the *man*. Proposition J. He is the principal plank on our platform. He is on the banner that goes before us in war. He is here with us on the right. We sealed him up in our positions, our rallies, our wars, our politics and our mass mailings. We've got him . . . we've dressed him up in prejudice. Made him hate the poor, the immigrant, and Mickey Mouse. He speaks very little . . . we talk for him."

And I hear a voice from the left, "We *really do* have Jesus because Jesus is 'down for the cause,' but we've stripped him of most of his power, his glory, and his mystery. We made Jesus another great teacher, a nonviolent freedom fighter—you know like Gandhi, or Martin, or Nelson. We made Jesus more manageable. We've got him under control."

It did not dawn on Mary that nobody took Jesus. She did not realize Jesus got up and got out of there himself. The living Christ does not dwell long where death is. Death is not a lifestyle for him; it is simply a portal to new life. She didn't know that Jesus had come forth from death to usher in a new and living way.

Mary couldn't conceive that Jesus could be doing such a radical new thing. She loved him but she couldn't imagine the full scope of his power and influence.

She did not know that he could steal victory from his own death and ours. She did not know that she need not pity the Sovereign God, the One who is the resurrection. Mary couldn't imagine that death had been turned into life . . . and once the dead ones had tasted life again *no* grave could hold them.

There are those of us who would prefer a dead Christ in his place to a living one outside of our control. There are those who can only recognize Christ in certain forms and under certain circumstances.

Imagine the struggle for some quiet Protestant church folks watching some African American folks dancing in the spirit well into the night. I'm sure someone felt the need to ask the question, "How dare these people try to claim my Jesus? They may have a Jesus, but it is not my Jesus. I've got a picture right here to prove it."

Imagine a group of patriarchal religious folks watching a group of men, women, and children who are not gender or orientation limited rejoicing in their Savior in perfect freedom? I'm sure someone would say, "What have they done with our Jesus? Surely he would not condone what I can't condone."

Can we hold Jesus in our religions?

Can we keep Jesus in our churches?

Can we even confine him to Christianity?

Into what sect, denomination, movement, or order has Jesus crowded all the riches of heaven? Into which race, ethnicity, country, culture, gender, or orientation has Jesus poured out all of himself exclusively? To whom has he given all the truth so that we may cease to seek him daily?

He's up from the dead now, out of the confines of the tomb . . .

He's out of the grave now and he will not be held exclusively, by anyone.

Just about the time we feel we have Jesus down to a science we see the wonder of his ability to show up in people and in places we never would have guessed possible. He is alive and he is still speaking.

If we seek to confine him behind any walls, any stone, he will break out every time.

He is the living way.

He is the living truth.

He is a fresh flowing river.

He is resurrection power.

He is light and he is life.

STIR UP THE GIFT

2 Timothy 1:1–7

> I am reminded of your sincere faith, a faith that lived first in your grandmother Lois and your mother Eunice and now, I am sure, lives in you. For this reason I remind you to rekindle the gift of God that is within you through the laying on of my hands: for God did not give us a spirit of cowardice, but rather a spirit of power and of love and of self-discipline. (2 Tim. 1:5–7)

PAUL EXPRESSES HIS LOVE for the young Timothy in his letter and reminds Timothy of his roots. All of us have roots, and there are some qualities we have, good and bad, that we inherited. I am glad God helps us to profit from the good and overcome the bad. We also have gifts, which we inherited. We have gifts that we discovered, gifts that were poured into us by mentors and teachers and some that we are actively cultivating. But Paul is talking to Timothy about the gift of God *placed* in Timothy by God.

Apparently some thing or some string of things has caused Timothy's gift to die down. It is there, but barely distinguishable.

Paul is encouraging the young Tim to *stir it up*.

The metaphor literally means to kindle anew the flames of fire . . . to shake the ashes off the God-given fire that is already in you so a new blaze of fire can be clearly seen.

How do you rekindle fire?

I love our church camping trips, and one of my traditional tasks has been to build the bonfire at the end of the day, when the cool of the evening begins. I have subsequently had a great deal of experience building fires over the years, and I have wonderful memories of our times of fellowship around those fires.

Building and sustaining a good fire requires work. There are some things that have to be done when a fire dies down in order to build it up again to be a place of warmth or to provide another of the many services fire performs for us.

Stir it up: You cannot stand off from a fire that has died down and command it to flame up. You must get involved with it. Move it around, see what is there, and assess what is needed. Move the hot embers together and get them prepared. Knock the ashes off to reveal the hot spots. Challenge yourself. Search around internally and externally for your gifts. Tune up your ear to listen for the voice of God revealing God's plan and purpose for your gifts. Tune out those voices and choices that stand in opposition to the voice and will of God for you. Find your creativity again . . . dream again . . . vision again. Don't let traditional things be a barrier to stirring up the gift of God in you— things like age, time, physical disability, and lack of resources. Your destiny is in those coals. They are still burning, passion is still there; you just need to shake off the ashes and stir it up.

Add fuel to it: You must feed a fire to start it burning hot again. Fire needs fuel but you have to add your fuel carefully . . . a little paper or straw, some kindling next, and then, when it is going good, add the larger logs. Big projects and plans that begin without steady underlying consecration, thought, and prayer are like throwing a big log on the fire without enough kindling underneath. The big log smolders, but it will not burn. Fire is at once useful and dangerous. Certain things when added to fire will cause it to burn out of control. Choose the things you use for your fire carefully—what you see, what you read, what kinds of conversations you participate in can determine the quality of your fire or the formation of your gift. Also it will not do to build it up big and roaring and think it will burn indefinitely by itself. Yesterday's kindling and logs were for yesterday. Keep an eye on your fire, protect it and watch the character of it, what feeds it, what works and what doesn't. Become intimate with the gift of God in you. Honor it and add some fresh fuel to it daily; minister to your gift according to the need.

Keep watch over it: If a fire is to continually burn it must be attended to. Don't wait until you notice you are cold. Sitting with my back to the bonfire, I could tell when the fire was getting too low. I got cool . . . cool leads to cold . . . cold indicates a dead fire. When my back registered "cool" I knew it was time to turn around and attend to the fire and determine what was needed to get it going again. I would have to interrupt my conversation, or stop playing a game, but the fire required it. You see, if the fire died everyone in my immediate vicinity would be affected. Pay attention to the fire. Appreciate the fact that the original flame, the original gift, came from God. God is making you responsible to steward over it. Don't take it for granted. God gives the fire . . . we tend it. Tend it like it is precious and priceless. Don't be afraid to say, "No, I can't do that or I can't go there, it will disturb my fire."

Use it: Fire has purpose and we tend to take better care of it when we use it. The fire in the hearth in homes in our past was a place where the entire clan received warmth. It was a place of gathering because after a cold, mean, indifferent day everyone's heart turned toward home and hearth. A good meal was cooked there. Hot water for a warm drink was prepared there. The rocking chair was right in front of the hearth for comfort. The fire even produced light so the family could read in the evening. Your gift is not for you alone. It was given for you to share it and to bless others with it. Use it. There is much more to the gift of God in us than we can imagine.

After Paul reminded Tim about his gifts, he told him that God has laid the foundation for the gifts to come forth. Paul started with what God did not give us.

God did not give us fear. Fear is torment and paralyzes the gift of God by waving the specter of failure over us. A fear-based relationship to God or the gift of God stifles creativity. Fear asks, "Will I be appreciated, will I be accepted, am I as good as the other people who do this?"

This is why we must change our motivation. Paul told the saints, "In all that you do, do it for God." You focus less on failure when you offer your gift to God first. We minister to God by ministering to the people.

God has laid the foundation for the gifts to come forth by being the one who gives first. What has God given us? Power, love, a sound mind, courage, sensitivity, good sense, strength, charity, and self-discipline.

Power, courage, and strength alone can be devastating, selfish and destructive. Love, sensitivity, and charity can be sentimental, codependent, and misdirected. A sound mind, good sense, and self-discipline can be self righteous, academic, and analytical. But together these qualities temper each other and are the foundation for our gifts to come forth and enable us to do great exploits for God!

Stir up those gifts, reach out again for your destiny without fear and with full assurance of faith, knowing that God's Spirit will grant the power, love, and self-discipline to accomplish it.

THE FIGHT TO FIT IN

Acts 21:17–32, 35–36

When we arrived in Jerusalem the brothers received us warmly. The next day Paul went with us to visit James; and all the elders were present. After greeting them, he related one by one the things that God had done among the Gentiles through his ministry. When they heard it they praised God. Then they said to him, "You see, brother, how many thousands of believers there are among the Jews, and they are all zealous for the law. They have been told that you teach all the Jews living among the Gentiles to forsake Moses, and that you tell them not to circumcise their children or observe the customs." (Acts 21:17–21)

THE JEWISH SAINTS WHO HAD CONVERTED and become disciples of Christ swelled the ranks of the Jerusalem church. But there was a problem. They believed in Christ but were still "zealous for the law" (v. 20). This was a difficult time for the young Christian church in transition from the law to grace. They were working it out by the day. "What do we keep of the old ways and what do we let go?" Rumors had reached these

Hebrew Christians that Paul, the apostle to the non-Jewish believers, or Gentiles, was telling the Jews who lived among the Gentiles to forsake the law of Moses, encouraging them not to circumcise their children and not to keep the customs of Israel. Paul was overwhelmingly successful in leading people to Christ, Jew and Gentile alike. The people who should have rejoiced with Paul over the success of his ministry became concerned that Paul's teaching was not carrying forth Jewish customs.

Paul had returned to Jerusalem. He had left behind him the many churches in Asia Minor, Macedonia, and Greece. He had faced enormous suffering, prison, beatings, and shipwrecks. Many souls were added to the church because of Paul's witness and preaching. He was coming to Jerusalem to celebrate this glorious victory with the saints.

Paul went before James and the elders to testify about the move of God during his missionary journeys. There was brief praise and rejoicing. There was a long criticism and admonition. He was directed to go and take the Nazarite vow—fasting, abstinence from drinking, sponsoring some young acolytes, and so on—to indicate his loyalty to the law of Moses . . . so he can be accepted . . . and he did it.

The need to be a part, to be accepted in a community of the beloved, is a powerful human need. Paul agreed to perform a ritual, go through some motions to prove himself worthy of acceptance. He submitted to a system of beliefs that were in truth not working for him anymore. He knew there was no salvific value in the ritual. Paul had seen God move powerfully, often to his amazement, in cultures other than his.

Paul was nearly beaten to death in spite of his efforts to fit in when he was recognized as one who previously brought a Gentile into the temple. He was beaten because he had become unintentionally different. He is a man marked as an agent for change. He was crossing over into a new and living covenant and he was called to bring the world, Jew and Gentile, slave and free, with him.

Paul was delivered from the vigilantes determined to destroy him by those he was sent to minister to: the Gentiles. He spoke their language. As God's agent for change, he stood between what was and what is coming. This is a place of great struggle, great courage, and great victory. Paul came to understand God as his defender, his protector, and his safe harbor. Paul learned a great lesson that day. He did not need to compromise his present truth to be accepted. Trying to do so was a waste of time. When God moves you to a higher level of understanding there is no turning back. The blessing lies ahead. There is no going back.

God had said some things in ages past, but God was speaking something new. Paul was accepted and acceptable to God and he was fulfilling his destiny and call in spite of the rejection he experienced in the presence of his beloved. Paul went on to finish his course and left us the immeasurable gift of chronicling his journey. What point are you trying to prove to those who criticize your call and destiny?

My grandfather once shared a parable with me that says, "If you have a dollar in your pocket, and someone says you don't have a dollar, resist the temptation to pull it out and prove it. Those who don't believe you have a dollar will not believe it even if they see it. They will call it fake money. Just wait . . . rub on the dollar in your pocket and just wait until spending time comes. When they see you with a bag full of candy they will know your money was real."

Don't worry that your part doesn't fit now. Some are called to the road less traveled and not to the beaten path. I used to play clarinet in our school orchestra, and a clarinet can make a horrible sound when it hits an "off" note. The only way it can be made right would be if the whole song changed key and the note became a part of something new. God is still speaking and the songs are changing key . . . follow the voice and leading of the living God and the living way!

JUNETEENTH

John 8:31–36, 2 Corinthians 5:16–21

Then Jesus said to the Jews who had believed in him, "If you continue in my word, you are truly my disciples; and you will know the truth, and the truth will make you free." They answered him, "We are descendants of Abraham and have never been slaves to anyone. What do you mean by saying, 'You will be made free'?" Jesus answered them, "Very truly, I tell you, everyone who commits sin is a slave to sin. The slave does not have a permanent place in the household; the son has a place there forever. So if the Son makes you free, you will be free indeed." (John 8:31–36)

From now on, therefore, we regard no one from a human point of view; even though we once knew Christ from a human point of view, we know him no longer that way. So if anyone is in Christ, there is a new creation: everything old has passed away; see, everything has become new! (2 Cor. 5:16–17)

WE ARE CELEBRATING JUNETEENTH, the day that commemorates Major General Gordon Granger's announcement in Galveston, Texas, that the war was over and the slaves were free. He brought an announcement that Texas called "General Order Number 3" and it read:

> The people of Texas are informed that in accordance with a Proclamation from the Executive of the United States, all slaves are free. This involves an absolute equality of rights and rights of property between former masters and slaves, and the connection heretofore existing between them becomes that between employer and free laborer.

This announcement came to Texas June 19, 1865, two years after President Lincoln's Emancipation Proclamation, which had become official January 1, 1863.

Some suggest that the messenger who was bringing the news in 1863 was killed, and some say that the news was withheld because the Texas plantation owners wanted to keep it from the slaves as long as possible to bring in as many crops as possible before the southern economy collapsed. But many states, parishes, and counties had been excluded from learning of President Lincoln's Emancipation Proclamation, leaving millions of African American slaves without their freedom. During the Civil War, Texas did not experience any significant invasion by Union forces. Although the Union army made several attempts to invade Texas, they were thwarted by Confederate troops.

As a result, slavery in Texas continued to thrive. In fact, because slavery in Texas experienced such a minor interruption in its operation, many slave owners from other slave-holding states brought their slaves to Texas to wait out the war. News of the emancipation was suppressed due to the overwhelming influence of slave owners. Granger's General Order Number 3 finally freed some eight hundred thousand slaves in Texas whose bondage, due to the minimal Union presence in the region, had been essentially unaffected by Lincoln's efforts. June 19—which was quickly shortened to "Juneteenth" among celebrants—has become the African American addendum to the national Independence Day, for, as Juneteenth jubilees remind us, the Emancipation Proclamation did not bring about emancipation, and the prevailing portrayal of Independence Day ignores the reality of slavery entirely.

When the slaves heard about their freedom many immediately left the fields and plantations, heading north where they heard that more opportunities existed . . . but many also remained behind.

How do you keep a slave a slave when freedom has come?

How do you manage to keep someone languishing in such a hateful institution from grasping such important information?

I propose two ways:

- You make him or her believe he or she is not actually a slave so freedom does not apply to him or her, or

- You keep him or her from knowing he or she has been set free.

Jesus addresses the first of these blindnesses to freedom in the John passage. He speaks to the folks who by virtue of their religion and culture felt they had no need for freedom from slavery—slaves who don't see themselves as slaves.

Essentially Jesus said, "You don't think this freedom I am offering applies to you, so let's cut to the chase. If you sin at all you are sinners in need of a savior. You cannot free yourself from the practice or penalty of sin. You are a slave to it and you will never get free with good works, good bloodline, and religious piety. You must be set free, because you are a slave to it, and all have sinned and are at present coming short of the glory of God (v. 37). You are a slave and although you think your place is secure, it is not, because you are not sons and daughters. It takes the Son to set the slave free. And the Son wants to not only set you free but to see that you are adopted into the family of God."

The second blindness to freedom is truly insidious because it is often perpetuated by religion. It is found in Paul's second letter to the Corinthians, chapter 5, verses 17–19. We are free because God in Christ is not counting our trespasses against us. And God has gone a step further and has made us ministers of reconciliation, much like Harriet Tubman, who after she was free came back and got three hundred of her sisters and brothers. But you won't seek to set anyone else free until you know you are free. What hinders us from knowing we are free?

People, society, and religion keep the news from us and keep us working on trying to free ourselves. It creates a slave pool for religion made up of people always struggling but never acquiring freedom and therefore in constant need of the religious machine to provide them with a method to earn their salvation. Religion tells us we are to work to earn our salvation much like an indentured servant worked to earn freedom. Religion does not truly celebrate the fact that we are freed by the work that Jesus did, not by the works that we do. Our works are our grateful response to his work.

It is too wonderful to grasp. That we are truly justified by faith, not by works of the flesh or religious acts. The qualitative life that follows is in direct response to God empowering us to make positive change, but we are fully received by God without changing anything at all. Salvation is by faith alone . . . period. Thank God, God had sense enough not to leave the saving or the sustaining of our salvation in our hands. It is too precious a thing for unpredictable beings like ourselves, who are subject to emotional highs and lows. Jesus died for this salvation. It did not come cheaply, and if it were left to us to manage it we would likely love what God hates, and hate what God loves . . . we would reject those whom God embraces, and think we were right when we were wrong. We would believe we are strong when we are weak, because our thoughts are often as far from God's thoughts as east is from west. Faith in the finished work of Calvary must stand alone as the path to salvation.

If we are to be freedom bringers we must know and acknowledge our own freedom. How do you look the day after you find out you are free? Just like you looked the day before, but something has passed away and something has become new. It is a change of status and position. The Granger Proclamation said the slaves were no longer bound by the master/servant model but by the employer/laborer model. In our new model we are the children of God. If you don't acknowledge it, you cannot walk in it.

Someone needs a proclamation of freedom. Take out a piece of paper. Write *Freedom* on it and give it to your sister or brother. Tell that person:

"This news may be late getting to you, but the war is over and we are no longer slaves to anything. Jesus has set us free and we are free indeed. God has sent a full regiment of angels to enforce your freedom and to guard you from the enemy. Now walk in your freedom, give the news to others and set people free everywhere you go!"

The Upper Room

Acts 1:4–8,12–14, 2:1–2

Then they returned to Jerusalem from the mount called Olivet, which is near Jerusalem, a Sabbath day's journey away. When they had entered the city, they went to a room upstairs where they were staying, Peter, and John, and James, and Andrew, Philip and Thomas, Bartholomew and Matthew, James son of Alphaeus, and Simon the Zealot, and Judas son of James. All these were constantly devoting themselves to prayer, together with certain women, including Mary the mother of Jesus, as well as his brothers. (Acts 1:12–14)

When the day of Pentecost had come, they were all together in one place. And suddenly from heaven there came a sound like the rush of a violent wind, and it filled the entire house where they were sitting. (Acts 2:1–2)

OUR STORY OPENS with a group of Jesus' disciples in a room waiting for something that Jesus called "'power from on high." This ambiguous power experience was to enable them to be great witnesses, and the command from Jesus after he ascended was for them to return to their upstairs rented room in Jerusalem and wait for it. Eleven disciples, now minus Judas, the women, the Marys and Joanna, Jesus' brothers, and those who believed, such as Nicodemus and Joseph of Arimathea—120 in all—were there, waiting.

PREPARATION FOR THE COMING OF THE SPIRIT

In my Pentecostal upbringing much emphasis was placed on the coming of the Holy Ghost but not on what transpired while the disciples waited for it. What was really going on among these believers? Graduation is wonderful, but the education that leads to graduation is the object of the experience . . . in the long run education makes graduation pale in comparison. Perhaps the preparation for the event was much more significant than the event itself. They waited together in the same room for ten days. What if the waiting afforded them the opportunity for reconciling relationships? These disciples had issues with each other and I can visualize them initially going to different parts of the room with the group and leader they most identified with. Here they were, stunned by the recent events, without the physical presence of their Teacher and with a commandment from Jesus to wait for power but not really know what to expect. On top of all of this . . . they had issues!

I suspect they had been so focused on the oppression from the outside, that they had little time to look critically at the issues they had among them and the things that divided them. I believe they were not unlike us—church folk—and church folk under stress can be a challenge. There had been much competition among the disciples, a lot of jockeying for power, and the residue of criticism must have still been in the air. There had been jealousy regarding some of them being too close to Jesus. Peter had denied Jesus three times in one night, had left, had gone back to fishing, and had now returned.

Thomas had doubted the resurrection until he saw the wounds on Jesus' body. James and John had argued with the others over who was greatest and who would have which position in Jesus' kingdom. There might have been some bad feelings between Jesus' family and the disciples regarding the rightful passing of authority.

Jesus had left John responsible for Mary, Jesus' mama, and she had other sons. Imagine that dynamic. In the mix of waiting disciples were those Gentiles whom Jesus had touched and I am sure this caused some consternation among the Jewish believers. Now Mary Magdalene with her suposedly spurious past was on her own without Jesus to cover her. What about the Pharisee Nicodemus? Could he be trusted? After all, he was a member of the Sanhedrin. He was from headquarters. And Joseph who gave his tomb—he was rich and therefore automatically suspect.

Church folk with church folk issues, waiting for the promise of power . . . for ten days they waited, together in one room.

I believe that the Spirit could have fallen as soon as they arrived but the process would have been thwarted. That's why Jesus sent them upstairs to wait. I am sure someone wondered, "Why didn't Jesus just give the blessing. What is all this waiting about?" That's where the church is today. Celebrating our denominations, appreciating our histories, performing our rituals and our baptisms, each one in his or her corner of the room waiting for power yet needing to reconcile ourselves to each other and our God.

I wonder what would happen if every city church as we know it was put on hold and we were closed up in one place for ten days—no structure, no liturgy, no one in charge, no order except for the word from Jesus to wait until we receive the power of the Holy Ghost. How long would it take us to take off our religion and become relational? What kinds of issues would arise for us? To which group in which corner of the room would we all go?

Someone said, well, that's simple. We are all on the same page.

Are we? And what page is that? What power struggles would be revealed in our waiting? What issues of superiority would emerge? What would be our collective goal? What efforts would we put all of our energy behind, even if they were someone else's ideas? What grudges would we need to drop? What Gentiles would we need to receive? Who would we need to forgive? Who would need to forgive us? How would we handle homophobia, xenophobia, classism, racism, sexism, and all the other phobias and isms?

Someone said the coming of the Spirit took care of all of that in the upper room, but I believe that the Spirit was poured out when the folks started moving out of their corners and cliques and seeking to find ways to be with one accord.

The greatest manifestation of the power of God comes when we work together to find ways to be together and do justice together and love together and stand together.

In 1906 in Los Angeles a revival broke out in a small mission on Azusa Street, led by Rev. William J. Seymour. This revival marked the beginning of the modern day Pentecostal movement. The event has been reduced over time to a group of people displaying external "signs and wonders" such as speaking in tongues, healings, and prophecy, with little meaning to most people today. But the power of that Pentecostal revival was not in the external manifestations of speaking in tongues and healings but in the miracle of black and white people worshipping together, men and women preaching together and decrying racism and sexism by their very presence in one place. The Spirit still moves when we move past our prejudices and differences.

And when they were with one accord in one place there came sound, a rushing mighty wind, the wind of the Spirit that brings life to dry bones, and the fire of the Spirit that illuminates the shadows where some used to dwell, and the tongues . . .

The tongues came to make the message of the love of Jesus understood to everyone. We all need to hear it in a way we can understand it.

'Cause everybody ought to know who Jesus is. Our challenge is not how to receive the Spirit, but rather how to receive each other, so the Spirit can freely come!

The Altar and the Tent

Genesis 12:1–8

> Now the LORD said to Abram, "Go from your country and your kindred and your father's house to the land that I will show you. I will make of you a great nation, and I will bless you, and make your name great, so that you will be a blessing. I will bless those who bless you, and the one who curses you I will curse; and in you all the families of the earth shall be blessed." . . . Then the LORD appeared to Abram, and said, "To your offspring I will give this land." So he built there an altar to the LORD, who had appeared to him. From there he moved on to the hill country on the east of Bethel, and pitched his tent, with Bethel on the west and Ai on the east; and there he built an altar to the LORD and invoked the name of the LORD. (Gen. 12:1–3, 7–8)

WHAT DO YOU DO when you feel that urge from God to make real changes in your life? You know, that deep sense of "I need to be busy doing the will of God . . . being productive in God's realm." It gets in your night dreams and day visions. "I hear you calling me, God, to move up, to break through the barriers and claim my destiny and your promise. So I'm going to make that move. I've packed my stuff and I'm sitting on my suitcase waiting for your direction."

Abraham had such an experience with God. I believe he was hit by that itch as God was grooming him for his destiny. Abraham, or Abram, as he was called before the full vision was revealed, was in Haran with his family and living a seemingly peaceful nomadic way of life when the call for great change came.

God spoke, "Get up, pack up, and go." I don't know if Abram asked what would be a logical question to me. "Where might we be going, God?" According to the story God gave the following directions, solicited or not, "Go to the land where I send you." So Abram gathered his family, his flocks, and his people . . . headed up and moved out for the strange land that this strange God was leading him to. And when he reached it he was given a great promise and a new name.

And Abraham was filled with joy and gratitude in this new place with such new promise. A fresh opportunity and an exciting future. Abraham built God an altar to signify his gratitude, worship, adoration, and submission. He needed this place sanctified as praying ground. A place where he could return to get fresh direction on this mysterious journey. The presence of this altar was a symbol of the presence of God in the camp. Abraham built an altar . . . then he built his tent.

I began to see the trend. Abraham and later his son Isaac worshipped or built altars to God in the same place where they set up house. The altar and the tent were always together. The altar calls for the tent, and the tent calls for the altar.

The altar is where we worship, submit, and respond to the will of God for our lives. The altar is where we spend our personal time with God, where we acknowledge our need for the abiding tangible presence of God in our camp. It is vitally important that we stay close to God in times of great transition and transformation, as our emotions are raw and vulnerable in this season of our lives.

The tent is where we live our lives, interact with family, church, and other people, do our tasks, serve and minister God's love. The tent connects us to this world, this cosmos. Abraham's altar consumed a burnt offering as a representation of himself offered up to God. He did this first before he set up his tent. He prayed there and sought God's will before setting up housekeeping.

How can we live a life that builds an altar before a tent? What things do we need to lay on the altar before we set up our tents? How would our lives be different if we put everything on the altar of sacrifice and allowed God to consume what God did not want us to take into our tents? I am certain that some of the things we have in our camp would never have made it if we had stopped at the altar first.

The altar keeps our tents from getting cluttered.

We no longer lay animals on the altar but we can place there the essence of ourselves, our plans and goals, our ideas about the future, our careers, our finances, our loves, and our relationships. The call to great change often comes in parts. You can get the *where* but not the *when*. You get the *who* but not the *how* . . . the *what* but not the *why*. Put your great vision and great passion on the altar and wait for a revelation of where to place your feet before taking off with a partial understanding. Don't bypass the altar and have a tent full of sorrow. The altar calls for the tent and the tent calls for the altar. In all thy ways acknowledge God and God will direct your paths. Amen.

LAZARUS LIVES
(THIS DEATH WILL NOT KILL YOU)

John 11:1–44, 12:9–11

> Now a certain man was ill, Lazarus of Bethany, the village of
> Mary and her sister Martha. Mary was the one who anointed
> the Lord with perfume, and wiped his feet with her hair; her
> brother Lazarus was ill. So the sisters sent a message to Jesus,
> "Lord, he whom you love is ill." But when Jesus heard it, he
> said, "This illness does not lead to death; rather it is for God's
> glory, so that the Son of God may be glorified through it."
> (John 11:1–4)

WHEN JESUS HEARD LAZARUS was sick, he tarried. He did not go to
Bethany, but stayed where he was, seemingly on purpose. And he made
this strange statement . . . strange for him who knows all things. He
said, "This illness does not lead to death" (v. 4). Then when questioned
in verse 14, Jesus says Lazarus is dead. And Lazarus did die . . . Jesus let
him die. Jesus stayed away intentionally until his friend died. Jesus knew
this was a death that would not end in death, but in life.

Jesus said the death was necessary so that God through him could be glorified. When is death necessary to glorify God and why didn't Jesus come and save his friend? I can recall having tragedy in my life that I thought Jesus could have, no, should have prevented only to find out later that God knows what is really best for me.

Often I have refused to let go of things and situations that needed to die and it felt as if Jesus stayed away until there was no visible sign of life in the things I wanted to hold on to. Had I been given the opportunity I would have kept them on life support indefinitely.

It was the custom of the Jews that the eldest son or next of kin closes the eyes of the dead and binds the mouth. The death is announced and the mourners begin to wail with a loud voice. They then wash the body and anoint it with ointments to retard decomposition. When Jesus died Nicodemus and the women brought a mixture of myrrh and aloes weighing a hundred pounds.

Ointments notwithstanding, the dead would stink and become unbearable because of the hot sun. You know when a thing is dead because it stinks.

No matter how much perfume you put on death, it stinks. No matter how close you may have been to someone, when they pass away you would be considered a severely emotionally disturbed person if you sat them up in your living room. You would not have friends; people would not visit you, and in time the things that colonize a dead body would begin affect your living body. We are often not convinced that God has initiated an end in order to bring about a beginning until we smell something . . . until it becomes clear that something has died. Jesus loved Lazarus and he let Lazarus die.

Death is necessary to bring about resurrection. To be resurrected to something new we must die fully. A seed must die to germinate and make a new plant grow. New life comes from death. This is the resurrection principle. Resurrection requires staying in the tomb alone for a time allowing people to mourn you as though there is little hope you will survive.

People of the resurrection die often, but new life must come from death or death will become unbearable. If we believe in Jesus, although we are dead, yet we shall live.

At the time of death there is mourning and grief until Jesus takes over (v. 34–38). Some say, "What can even Jesus do with a decomposing body?" Maybe when it was freshly dead there was a chance that it was a coma or a seizure and not really death . . . but not now, now that it stinks and death is certain.

Victory comes when Jesus takes over in the midst of the stench of our lives and speaks life to our deadness. Come forth, come forth and live.

Something brand new was coming alive in Lazarus. Something was coming to life although so much was dead. Lazarus heard Jesus through his deadness. And Jesus was calling his name, "Lazarus, get up, my friend." Lazarus knew that voice. Way down in the darkness of that tomb he heard Jesus. One eye popped open, one leg wiggled, the decomposition process was moving from the inside to the outside of his body; the stench moved from Lazarus' body to his grave clothes. He was becoming new from the inside out.

Lazarus, the deadness that was in you is now just on your clothes. The ointments and resins have mixed with the body fluids and formed a smelly casing for your body. You still smell dead but it is superficial. The smell is in your grave clothes.

The people had bound him in grave clothes for his burial. Lazarus' life was under the bondage of people who did what they did because they believed it was right and it was the custom. But the clothes of a dead man now hindered Lazarus and the same people that had bound him had to set him free. Jesus told them to loose him from his grave clothes.

If we want to see resurrection life manifested through us and our churches today we must participate in "loosing" people Jesus has set free . . . moving the barriers and bonds we have put on folks even if we thought we were doing the right thing in binding them. Three thousand and five hundred people were added to the church on the day of Pentecost because the disciples preached one Jesus in many tongues. We preach too many different Jesuses and too many ways to get to him and too many ways to be after we get him that are based on our cultural and theological location. This is how we bind people. We have a Holiness Jesus, and a Baptist Jesus, a black Jesus, and an uptown Jesus and a poor folks' Jesus. Our Jesus loves what we love and hates what we hate. We bind people instead of loosing them. If the Son has set them free we need to do the same thing. "Loose him," Jesus said, and he is saying it still.

The resurrection of Lazarus drew people to God and the resurrection principle still draws people to the church because it is life. Dying and dead people want to live. If we want effectiveness in ministry individually and collectively we have to stop trying to resuscitate dead things. Don't be afraid of death . . . it can't kill you. It is an opportunity for new life to begin.

Have the courage to let dead things die a natural death. Let it go. Trust the Lord in the tomb. He is the resurrection. There is a radical new thing in you that wants to come to life. There is radical new vision in us that is pleading to come to life.

Listen, Jesus is calling you by your name in the midst of your depression, your lack of enthusiasm, and your deadness. Jesus is saying, "I want you to come forth, but as someone brand new. Rise up and live!"

13

THE CONVERSION OF A PHARISEE

Acts 9:1–26

> Meanwhile Saul, still breathing threats and murder against
> the disciples of the Lord, went to the high priest and asked
> him for letters to the synagogues at Damascus, so that if he
> found any who belonged to the Way, men or women, he
> might bring them bound to Jerusalem. Now as he was going
> along and approaching Damascus, suddenly a light from
> heaven flashed around him. He fell to the ground and heard a
> voice saying to him, "Saul, Saul, why do you persecute me?"
> He asked, "Who are you, Lord?" The reply came, "I am Jesus,
> whom you are persecuting. But get up and enter the city, and
> you will be told what you are to do." The men who were trav-
> eling with him stood speechless because they heard the voice
> but saw no one. Saul got up from the ground, and though his
> eyes were open, he could see nothing; so they led him by the
> hand and brought him into Damascus. For three days he was
> without sight, and neither ate nor drank. (Acts 9:1–9)

IT WAS SIX DAYS from Jerusalem to Damascus. Saul had a mission. Saul
had a passionate determination to purge Israel of the followers of the

Way. How could this dead Galilean carpenter produce such an undaunted group of followers? Paul had just left Stephen's murder and he could not forget that look of absolute bliss on the martyr's face as he was stoned to death. What was wrong with these people? Their Jesus had been a political anarchist and a religious blasphemer and was rightfully crucified.

Saul had been appointed and given the enviable assignment by the leaders of the synagogue to rid his people of this false doctrine. He had papers that empowered him to drag Christians to Jerusalem for mock trials and imminent execution. He hated them anyway . . . all that love and singing and fellowship . . . so the purpose matched the prejudice. That made Saul a dangerous man.

He was the worse kind of righteous crusader; he actually kept the law that he enforced, which made him all the more self-righteous!

Paul, as his name became after his conversion, said of his life as a Pharisee, "I was blameless regarding the law." Saul had a conscience informed by legalism and not by grace and acceptance. He was committed to an impeccable obedience to the law and traditions of his people and intolerant of any one who did not keep that law. He was a resourceful scholar and a natural leader who was the son of elite Jews, was raised in the culture of Greece and Rome, was educated at the best schools, and learned theology at the feet of Gamaliel, the greatest teacher of Paul's time.

And worst of all he thought he was doing God a favor! He thought he was religiously right . . . Or did he? Was it possible that his head and heart were in moral conflict on that road? Is it possible he said, "I know these people are wrong according to the law but my heart is troubled about this Way. I've never experienced joy like these folk have or peace or fellowship. Yet how can this Way be the will of God? Is there something greater than the law of Moses?"

Was that the stinging prick he kicked against? Was he fighting the unanticipated prompting of the Holy Spirit ushering in a new dispensation? A movement in which Paul was to have a principle role?

Just as Saul needed reconciliation between his Jewish and Hellenistic backgrounds, God needed Paul to bridge the gap between the Hebrew Christians and Greek world, someone who could preach the liberating power of Jesus Christ! Saul had the training, but he could not become Paul until he encountered Christ.

He had to first be liberated. Before Saul/Paul could become a reconciler for the great issues of his time some things had to happen to him.

A CLEAR ENCOUNTER WITH JESUS CHRIST

It was Jesus that he persecuted when he persecuted the church. The followers of the Way were right; Jesus was alive and well! It was really Jesus that Saul was after anyway. Saul was angry with this teacher who loved Gentiles, women, children. This Jesus who flew in the face of tradition, who dared to call himself the Son of God. This Jesus whom common folk flocked to by the thousands; they would rather be with him than listen to the theological debates at the temple. This Jesus who was so secure in who he was that even death couldn't break him. I believe Saul really wanted what Jesus was giving away but he couldn't get past the rules of his religion. What a horrible internal struggle: to want Jesus but to miss Jesus because we can't get down off of our beast. I can't help but believe that this is what Paul wanted all along. If this Jesus is real, can he touch me, past my intellectual self; can he do something real in me? Can he help me translate my law into life?

INTELLECTUAL REMOLDING: SEEING THE LIGHT

The light shone all around him; no part was left unexposed. All of him was in the light and although it blinded his natural eyes his spiritual sensitivity was fully cognitive. The light is truth, and this truth was greater than Paul's head knowledge and his cultural fidelity. He saw Jesus not physically but with his perception, the way we "see" Jesus, and the light came on. It was a spectacular "ah-ha!" moment. Things were put in proper perspective. Priorities were rearranged. Saul saw Jesus. When Saul saw who Jesus was, he saw who Paul was to be.

CHARACTER TRANSFORMATION: FALLING OFF YOUR BEAST

Those whom Jesus calls to great works are laid low. It is the first real step toward advancement in Christ. We must learn to count as "dung" everything in comparison to the excellence of the knowledge of Christ. God could have finished the work on the road but there was a need to liberate this Pharisee from his hatred *and* to free the church from their fear of him. Saul's reputation preceded him and the saints knew the reason for his journey to Damascus. They feared him and God was directing them to do the unexpected for the undeserving so they might see the un-believable—a major risk. Brother Paul . . . where was the great Saul of Tarsus, so arrogant, resolute, powerful, now blind and helplessly de-pendent on those he came to destroy? Now Paul was being led into the very Damascus that he intended to purge. The purgor being cared for by the purgees. Ananias found a blind man praying where a killer used to be. Paul was stunned and disarmed by the kind, courteous, agape love of Jesus. Ananias lost his fear and Paul gained his sight and lived among the saints. Verse 20 says he immediately began to preach Christ.

God, show us the light and knock us from our beasts; blind us to the world until we pray, "God, what would you have me do?"

The Common Christ

Mark 1:9–11

> In those days Jesus came from Nazareth of Galilee and was baptized by John in the Jordan. And just as he was coming up out of the water, he saw the heavens torn apart, and the Spirit descending like a dove on him. And a voice came from heaven, "You are my Son, the Beloved; with you I am well pleased." (Mark 1:9–11)

THE SOUTHERN BAPTISTS FINALLY REPENTED to the African American community for their behavior during slavery and their denial of black folks' civil rights. Praise God! Jerry Falwell and Mel White finally sat down at meat after seven years together with some of the members of Falwell's church. One woman said she did not know SGL people were just people.

The UCC as the American Missionary Association confessed to the wrongful colonization of Hawaii, and the UCC pledged support for the sovereignty movement. These are hopeful signs that the body of Christ is coming around full circle.

The Christian church needs to come full circle and rediscover the common Christ. I love the narrative of Jesus' baptism by his cousin

John as recorded in the Book of Mark. In those days Jesus came from Nazareth of Galilee and was baptized by John in the Jordan. Simple. Uncomplicated. Jesus comes to his cousin, probably undressed to his loincloth, steps into the water, and is baptized. The Spirit rests in him as he comes up from the water, signifying God's pleasure with this moment. But as soon as he came up from the water we began to dress him up . . . and we have done it for the last two thousand years. We have dressed Jesus up in our rituals, traditions, and religions so much so that he is hardly recognizable. We are not really sure what it means to be Christlike. I visualize Jesus walking around bent over with layers and layers of rules on his back, carrying volumes and volumes of books and creeds in one hand, boxes of symbols, icons, and relics in the other with his layers of liturgical robes covered with blood shed in his name. Even the act of baptism itself has endured years of contentious debate—do we sprinkle, do we pour, is it for children, is it necessary for salvation, should it be done in Jesus' name or in the name of the Trinity? And the list goes on and on.

There are places and people that talk about Jesus, and their "Jesus talk" is completely foreign to the talk of other Christians. One place would hardly recognize the Jesus of the other place. When I was in Jerusalem and observed the orthodoxy of those who zealously watch over the shrines, I thought about how strange all the rituals, candles, incense, gold, and icons would be to my Pentecostal parents. I once heard a story about an older Baptist sister talking to the tour guide at the Sistine Chapel, as he was describing the intricacies of Michelangelo's ceiling masterpiece. She said. "Well all of that is well and good, but is any body getting saved here? It is a church, isn't it?"

We have completely divergent causes in the name of Christ. It has to be terribly confusing to seekers when we use the name Jesus and attach the name to issues that are completely at odds with each other. We cannot find a common cause because we don't have a common Christ.

If Christ has not changed, then how can he have such an identity crisis? How can he be the Jesus of the Roman Catholic Church and the Jesus of the Church of England? Is Jesus for the right or left? How can Jesus love us and despise us at the same time? How can he be the Jesus of the Grand Dragon of the Ku Klux Klan and the Jesus of Martin

Luther King Jr.? Jesus of the straight and gay? Why do the teachings attributed to Jesus differ so much from place to place? How does Jesus want us to live? What does Jesus want us to look like? Whom does Jesus want us to love? Whom does Jesus love and support?

I, like so many, once thought I knew exactly who Jesus was and is and what Jesus wanted. It was simple then and fell into three distinct categories: what Jesus loves, tolerates, and hates. It went something like this:

Jesus loves: straight people; people who go to church; people who don't lie, steal, or cuss; people who do not drink, or do drugs, except prescriptions. Jesus loves for us to have picnics and banquets. Jesus loves people who don't have sex until they are married; people who fast, pray, and suffer silently; people who obey leadership; compliant and obedient children, women, and black people; people who pay tithes; people who go to the meetings and convocations.

Jesus tolerates: bisexual people; Baptists, Methodists, and some Apostolics; people who don't come to church because they have to work on Sunday; people who cuss occasionally, especially men and deacons; occasional sex between saints, because two clean sheets can't dirty one another; those who don't join the twenty-one-day fast because of health concerns.

Jesus hates: openly SGL people; all non-Christian religions and Catholics; people who don't come to church at all; people who buy or sell sex; people who question or oppose leadership; people who have addictions to anything except food and clothes; all people who are really different from the rest of us and don't seem to show any desire to conform.

The question is, what part was Jesus and what part was us using Jesus to validate our culture? Where is the gospel in all of this? Where does culture and tradition stop and the way of Christ begin?

How can we begin to strip off the layers of stuff we have piled on Jesus to get to who he is? Where are the common denominators? How much pseudo-Christ will we lose to find a common Christ?

Somewhere in the midst of all of this junk is the real Jesus. Will someone help me undress him?

THE MOST UNLIKELY PLACE
FOR A CHURCH

1 Corinthians 1:26–31

Consider your own call, brothers and sisters: not many of you were wise by human standards, not many were powerful, not many were of noble birth. But God chose what is foolish in the world to shame the wise; God chose what is weak in the world to shame the strong; God chose what is low and despised in the world, things that are not, to reduce to nothing things that are, so that no one might boast in the presence of God. He is the source of your life in Christ Jesus, who became for us wisdom from God, and righteousness and sanctification and redemption, in order that, as it is written, "Let the one who boasts, boast in the Lord." (1 Cor. 1:26–31)

CORINTH: A city of almost seven hundred thousand souls. A city with two bustling harbors, with goods that flowed in and out from Italy, Spain, Asia Minor, Phoenicia, and Egypt. Although Corinth was not the university town that Athens was it was a center of Greek philosophy and wisdom.

Corinth was a city of love, where Aphrodite, the goddess of love, was at the top of the pantheon. The city boasted a thousand sacred prostitutes, men and women, who gave up any tie to family and career for the express purpose of sex for a price. The money was shared with the temple for temple upkeep.

Some would ask why would anyone want to establish a church in a city like Corinth—with all of the sin and debauchery going on there? Go inland to the suburbs where the agricultural people are . . . the calm, reasonable, normal, right-thinking people. But the Holy Spirit said I want a church in Corinth. Right in the middle of the madness, right at the center of town, made up of people from the edge.

Corinth strikes me as a marvelous location for a church. It sounds like a place where people would be ripe . . . not for religion, they had that already, but for relationship with the real love that comes from God in Jesus Christ. And the church was successful. The church at Corinth was one of the most successful churches founded by Paul. Now they had some issues: division in the church, incest, the saints suing each other, abuse of Christian freedom, chaos in worship services, marriage issues, and a new concept for Paul to deal with, strong women.

All of the issues you would expect from a community forming in "Aphroditeville" and one that knew very little about "appropriate church behavior." Corinth was a center of philosophy and wisdom, and the church included a former ruler of the synagogue, a city treasurer, and some successful business people; however, many of the members of the church were from the margins of society—socially, politically, and culturally.

There are those who would think that Paul's greatest pastoral challenge would be keeping these wayward people in line . . . and he did try in his letters to address the issues. I feel, however, that Paul's greatest challenge was not the morality of the believers at Corinth. That was a work that the Holy Spirit was and is active in, in the life of the believers. No, that was not the real danger. "But what about the incest case?" some might ask. "Surely that was a potential church killer!" Although it was inexcusable for that young man to sleep with his father's wife, when a community is made up of people from a culture where sex is worship and worship is sex, the fact that there was but one incident mentioned among the Corinthians is a living statement of the work of the Holy Spirit among them. They were being conformed to the image of Christ. Sometimes we forget that everyone's beginning point is not the same.

There was a greater danger.

God spoke to Paul through time and the prophet Jeremiah:

> Thus says the LORD: Do not let the wise boast in their wisdom, do not let the mighty boast in their might, do not let the wealthy boast in their wealth; but let those who boast, boast in this, that they understand and know me, that I am the LORD; I act with steadfast love, justice, and righteousness in the earth, for in these things I delight, says the LORD. (Jer. 9:23–24)

Paul echoed Jeremiah when he wrote to the Corinthians:

> [God] is the source of your life in Christ Jesus, who became for us wisdom from God, and righteousness and sanctification and redemption, in order that, as it is written: "Let the one who boasts, boast in the Lord." (1 Cor. 1:30–31)

The greater danger the church at Cornith faced was the potential dislocation of their boasting—giving up the "foolish" things that were powerful enough to bring them out of their former lives to embrace the wisdom of the more "respectable" culture. The danger was moving from boasting in God to boasting in themselves and their accomplishments as though those things happened apart from God.

Everyone desires to feel special, significant, and important. It is not hard, however, after a series of self-affirming accomplishments, to exchange gratefulness and humility for power, control, and boasting. The ink had hardly dried on the documents of independence written by the much-persecuted founders of this nation before they unapologetically took all the human, land, and mineral resources they could take from the natives of this land, and then took some of us from our native land. Boasting apart from God is dangerous stuff.

It is correct to give glory to God for deliverance from any oppression, and to be thankful to God for the wisdom and strength to choose the right counselor, therapist, doctor, treatment, and/or church where we can continue to grow.

It is quite another thing to think we achieved our successes and victories without God to help us. Humility is essential to achieving and sustaining our recovery from those things that would enslave us.

These Corinthians were thought of as scandalous. The first century term "to Corinthianize" meant to do any and every thing that brought pleasure no matter the cost. These were the people to whom the Holy Spirit sent Paul, to raise up a church.

The danger was not that they would not change but that they would change and fail to remember where to locate their boasting.

No one but God could take our shattered lives, pick up the pieces, and make us into vessels of honor . . . our boast is in God. No one but God could take our self-loathing and change us into someone we look in the mirror at and say, if I were not me I would be trying to date myself! Look what God has done . . . our boast is in God!

No one could take the ingredients we gave God and stir them up and make a community that shares and serves others . . . our boast is in the Lord!

We've got some land, and with God's help, we're going to get more.

We've got some cars, and with God's help, we're going to get more.

We've got our health back, and with God's help, our health will improve.

We've got hundreds and thousands of days of sobriety, and with God's help, we'll get thousands more.

We've got some joy and peace and love and we'll get more.

But let's be clear: our boast is not in our wisdom, in our strength, or in our riches . . . *Our boast is in our Sovereign God! Our God is an awesome God!*

CAN WE EAT TOGETHER?

Luke 14:16–24

> Then Jesus said to him, "Someone gave a great dinner party
> and invited many. At the time for the dinner he sent his slave
> to say to those who had been invited, 'Come; for everything is
> ready now.' But they all alike began to make excuses. . . . Then
> the master said to the slave, 'Go out into the roads and lanes,
> and compel people to come in, so that my house may be
> filled.'" (Luke 14:16–18, 23)

IN THE TRADITIONAL TELLING of this parable of Jesus, a feast is prepared, folks are invited, and then they are called the day of the event and
told that all things are now ready. The invitees beg off with various ex-
cuses and the servant responsible for notifying the guests is sent deeper
and deeper into the highways, hedges, streets, and lanes of the town to
find any willing person to come to the feast.

I have struggled with this interpretation that seems to imply that
the other, or the Gentile or the less fortunate, is welcome only as an
afterthought.

I have been rethinking this text and I have a question. Have you ever thought that there had to be a reason why nobody wanted to come to the feast? Can you imagine preparing a dinner and inviting a bunch of folks, getting a positive response from them, only to have them all decline the day of the supper? Was the initial invitation made publicly and the invitees did not have the heart to decline? Was the food typically poor or unimaginative or boring? Maybe we need to look again and see why it was so hard for the host to get these folks to come. It seems unlikely that everybody would come up with a lame excuse. Why is it that the only ones who took the messenger up on the invitation were clear across town, of another culture, of another orientation, or of another class? And he had to look hard to get any takers and then the messenger had to plead with them to come.

Where is the joy of the great feast that should have made it irresistible? When someone we all know can "sho nuff" cook puts on a feast, we get offended if we are left out. My associate pastor is an extraordinary cook and when we went camping one year she was frying some catfish in an open air cooking area. A European American brother was around the same area participating in a wine and cheese tasting. I noticed that he kept looking over at us and smiling. Finally his stomach took over the control of his feet and he came and asked the associate pastor for some fish. When he tasted it he swooned and told her that he had been trying to get his wife to learn how to fry fish like that, but she was not getting it. He wanted to know the recipe. She told him to go get some prepared fish fry mix because he just couldn't do everything we can do. When the fish was done she did not have to beg us to come. The smell alone pulled us from the whole campground with our plates, utensils, and stomachs ready.

What was it about this feast? Maybe this cook was too exotic; too multicultural. Maybe this cook prepared food that was just too much different to be comfort food for the folks on the invitation list. Try this on—perhaps Jesus was referring to a feast before its time, a prophetic feast. Uncomfortable food offered to people who wanted to be comfortable. Food designed to appeal to everyone even before the masses were welcomed to eat it. Imagine a discussion in the kitchen about how all people would be blessed by this feast without the commitment or the knowledge to get it out to the people who would benefit from it most. Food not desired by the folks on the list, but the list has not been changed to include the previously uninvited and unfamiliar dinner guests.

It is akin to amassing resources to do justice work without the faith to release those resources or having skills to assess the problem among people on the margin, then writing a position paper about it, but living in fear of the reprisals that would come from becoming personally involved with implementation.

Many folks don't like new stuff . . . new church . . . new worship.

We get concerned when certain words are connected to worship and church, words like awe and wonder, risk, unpredictability, lost control, Holy Ghost power . . .

What can make the feast welcoming to those who may not want to attend because they are wary of it, those who find the new fare too exotic, and those who have not been traditionally welcome? What about a feast of reconciliation? A feast where everyone is invited and where several kinds of foods are made available.

I believe the table of God must be a welcome table where liberal and conservative theologies can coexist and be heard. My grandmother used to think that every day should close with us eating together. No matter what our day was like, no matter what we were mad at each other about, we had to eat together. God's table, Jesus' table, should look like that. It would be a wonderful thing to behold, especially for me and folks like me who represent and constantly interact with people on the margins of many groups. I cling to a strong Christology and good old gospel music, I speak in tongues and have a personal relationship with Jesus, while I also believe in an educated clergy, a woman's right to choose and full rights for same gender loving people to marry and raise children. I am a Pentecostal traditionalist and a reconciling liberation theologian. It's like being a chittlin burrito with capers . . . so many things at one time; but I have a place at the feast of God. You can't keep me out 'cause it ain't your party, it's Jesus' party and we are all here by his invitation!

Here is the challenge: we are clear about what we disagree about but what about a table where we seek to find our intersections? Not an "either or" table but a "both and" table. What can be our great civil rights and human rights movement together? Any war is a civil war if we are truly one family of God. We can do justice and love and worship Jesus. Here is our great statement to the world about the great feast of God: all people, those in town, those from the highways, those from the hedges, those who are African, Native American, Asian, Latin, Irish, French, German, Dutch, Italian, Polynesian, Arab, Jew, Roma, Russian, Polish, English, Swedish, Norse, Turkish, Slavic, Danish, straight, gay, trans, bi, queer, intersex, rich, poor, Republican, Democrat, Independent, Green, tall, short, thin, fat, Christian, Jew, Muslim, Buddhist, Yoruba, young, old, disabled—all are welcome! What a great feast it would be! Imagine us humbly, hospitably, waiting for one another like Paul instructed the Corinthians at their celebration of the supper of remembrance. I dance; you dance. I eat; you eat. Get ready. God is doing a new thing. Don't miss it, for there is something at the table for you. God is still speaking . . . all of the words of this great invitation cannot be contained between the pages of a book. We are the demonstration of the invitation. Come over here, the table is spread and the feast of God is going on!

Does Anybody Want
to Dance with Me?

Exodus 15:19–27

When the horses of Pharaoh with his chariots and his chariot drivers went into the sea, the LORD brought back the waters of the sea upon them; but the Israelites walked through the sea on dry ground. Then the prophet Miriam, Aaron's sister, took a tambourine in her hand; and all the women went out after her with tambourines and with dancing. . . . When they came to Marah, they could not drink the water of Marah because it was bitter. . . . He (Moses) cried out to the LORD; and the LORD showed him a piece of wood; he threw it into the water, and the water became sweet. (Exod. 15:19–20, 23, 25)

GOD LED THE ISRAELITES to the Red Sea and to the Waters of Marah. Both were places of trial and testing. The Red Sea was a place of insurmountable hindrances and blocks. The waters of Marah was a place where the people were exceptionally tired and the provisions were low.

When they came to the Red Sea the sea stood before them and the powerful chariots of Ramses were behind them, but the story says that God divided the sea before them and they walked through on dry land. The old spiritual says, "Pharaoh's army got drown-ded in the Red Sea."

When they came to the waters of Marah after a three-day march from the sea, they were overwhelmed with thirst and found the waters horribly bitter and full of disease. God told Moses to pick up a piece of wood and cast it in to the waters. The waters became sweet and disease-free.

Here is a statement of faith and fact . . . God will divide our Red Seas and make the waters of Marah sweet for the children of God.

God moved the insurmountable hindrances and gave the people dry land victory. God provided what they had need of and gave them sweet water victory.

But the trials and victories are not what I want to focus on here. There will always be Red Seas and waters of Marah and we will cry out and God will hear us and bring us through.

A powerful thing happened between the Red Sea and Marah. Between the tests, Miriam led the children of Israel in a dance. I don't know how long the dance went on but the text says they had literal "foot service" where their instruments, hearts, and bodies danced before God.

When I hear the public voice of the church, there is too much lament, worry, anxiety, fear, grief, anger, debate, violence, sorrow, sadness, despair, and *not enough dancing. Does anybody want to dance with me?*

I wonder: do we ever listen to ourselves and the amount of energy we lend to the negative things in our lives? Church seems to be full of doom prophets and naysayers.

I saw a National Geographic special about how sand in the Serengeti desert takes over the green fertile land. The wind blows and bit by bit the sand moves in and smothers the life out of the green, lush, fruitful area until the land is more sand than soil. The crops cannot grow in sand. Most living things cannot thrive in sand. Are you allowing the struggles of your life to turn your soil to sand? Is the joy of your salvation ebbing away and being replaced by angst, cynicism, and fear? Is your hope lush and green or dry and dead? Where is the effervescence and evidence of the abundant life we talk so much about? *Does anybody want to dance with you?*

Something is out of balance when we permit our emotions to grieve and lament without permitting them to rejoice. Our praise ought to eclipse our lamentations. Our expectation of God's deliverance ought to be greater than our anticipation of trouble.

I can hear someone say, "Miriam had reason to dance . . . she had just come through the Red Sea." But Miriam was a prophet and knew she was in the desert with slavery behind her and great challenges before her.

I love the way the text reads. Moses raises up a long, beautiful, powerful, poetic praise for nineteen verses of the chapter 15 of Exodus, but Miriam snatched her tambourine and got some sisters together and danced before God as she sang to the congregation. Those sisters represented the ones most marginalized in their community . . . but they led the dance. Miriam's whole self was fully engaged in the praise. She abandoned herself to the praise. Her song said, "Sing to God, for God is *ga-ah*, *ka-bode* or highly elevated, majestic, gloriously exalted in triumph, weighted with honor, esteem, glory, abundance, and wealth. God has triumphed gloriously for us!"

Miriam grabbed her tambourine, the instrument consistently used in ancient times for worship music. When they saw her pick it up they knew the dance was on. She was letting the people know that it was time to praise God . . . not just time to talk about praise but to embody it. She was asking the question I am asking today—*does anybody want to dance with me?*

It is time for some Miriams to rise up and call forth a dance. The praise won't hurt you but it is death to the thing that is causing you to despair. The dance symbolizes the embodiment of praise. The dancing life is not passive. You have to constantly keep yourself reminded that you have the favor of God, the Sovereign God of all, and that God wants you to live the dancing life. God said through the prophet Isaiah that you can have your head covered with beauty, not ashes. Ashes are for mourning, sadness, and grief—not for those who have overcome.

God wants you to have the oil of gladness, not a spirit that mourns.

God wants you to have a garment of praise, not a spirit of heaviness.

Jesus died to do more than save us from eternal hell, but to free us from hell on earth. He died so we could live the dancing life.

Do the work of ministry, but keep dancing.

Fight the good fight of faith, but keep dancing.

Speak truth to power, but keep dancing.

Speak peace to war, but keep on dancing.

Bring provision to poverty, but keep dancing.

Look for a new job, but keep dancing.

Get counseling for your relationship, but keep dancing.

Work on your recovery from addictions, but keep dancing.

God is always to be highly exalted. God will always triumph gloriously, so nothing should hinder our dance.

Do you want to dance with me?

FORECAST OF PENTECOST
(WHO LET THE DOGS IN?)

Mark 7:24–30

> From there he (Jesus) set out and went away to the region of
> Tyre. He entered a house and did not want anyone to know he
> was there . . . but a woman whose little daughter had an un-
> clean spirit immediately heard about him, and she came and
> bowed down at his feet. Now the woman was a Gentile, of
> Syrophoenician origin. . . . He said to her, "Let the children
> be fed first, for it is not fair to take the children's food and
> throw it to the dogs." But she answered him, "Sir even the
> dogs under the table eat the children's crumbs." Then he said
> to her. "For saying that, you may go—the demon has left your
> daughter." (Mark 7:24–28)

PENTECOSTALISM HISTORICALLY BRINGS TO MIND mysticism, speaking
in tongues, healings, and receiving Holy Ghost power.

In Acts 1:8 it says that after the coming of the Holy Spirit the disciples would receive power . . . power to do what? Power to make the
message of Jesus accessible to everyone. Power to venture out geo-

graphically, culturally, and theologically. And though we often seek to do the work of Christ geographically, until we have ventured out and learned to respect another culture and theology our outreach is just a matter of imposing our religious ideas on other people. The real essence of Pentecost, which is to make the gospel understood and embraced by all people, has been in a geographical, cultural, theological, and denominational "girdle" for ages.

A girdle is a hateful thing, conceived in the mind of Satan and distributed to humankind, women in particular. It is a device of torture that has rolled up and rolled down, cutting off circulation and air supply. Many women who have allegedly passed out in church were probably victims of girdle constriction. It was a matter of trying to get too much in too small a space. Girdles have left lifelong battle scars upon us where metal, bone, and lycra spandex held this demonic device in place. Praise God for the invention of control top pantyhose and knee-high stockings!

In our text Jesus was in a tight place of transition. His culture was at war with his purpose, his nationality fighting with his universal call. Pentecost was in a girdle. The children Jesus referred to were his kin by blood, the Jews. The dogs were those who were of other origins and ethnicities. The "children" were not eating and the dogs were hungry.

He was a God-Man in a struggle—God extending the table to all, and man wanting to give priority to his own. My understanding of Jesus permits him to grow into his purpose. I don't believe he understood the entirety of God's will in him from the beginning, but rather his humanness lined up with his divinity over time.

He was in the region of Tyre and Sidon—Phoenician cities—present day Syria. He was on foreign soil, on purpose, and he did not want people to know he was there. He was among people who had other gods, their own kings, and their own coins and systems of government. He was traveling incognito. He went to Vegas.

He had just finished a big debate with the religious institutions back home and had debunked the idea that there was a distinction between clean and unclean meat. He was sick of church folks and taking a break and along came this woman who knew of his reputation as a healer. Her baby was sick and she meant to get some help for her child.

Jesus was about to be challenged internally with destroying the idea of clean and unclean people. Jesus the Jew was not truly at home with this concept. He was in a transition—his cultural prejudice was showing—he wanted to gather the Jews first as a mother hen does her chicks, but they would not fully receive him. He was not respected by the Jewish powers but he was not yet ready to be radically inclusive.

The Pharisees had branded him as a lawbreaker. He was regarded by Herod and Rome as a menace. He was being slighted by Nazareth, but yet he was not ready to accept this woman on equal terms with his people.

Jesus was seeking the seclusion of a foreign land to withdraw from the enmity of the Jews, but he was not in this land because he embraced these people—they wore the wrong clothes, danced to the wrong music, and worshiped the wrong gods.

But it was time to lay the foundation for Pentecost . . . it was coming . . . the blessing of the infilling of the Spirit with power to witness for Christ was to be available to all . . . and this woman, this "dog" was being used to break things open.

"Dog" was a contemptuous name that the Jews had for the Gentiles of this time. This woman was not referred to as a dog because of what she did, but simply for who she was.

Jesus' purpose needed this dog.

The church today needs some dogs to move it to its true purpose.

By running into this dog on his vacation Jesus was exposed to the faith of the Gentiles. She was not leaving without the blessing. Culture would not stop her, the disciples would not stop her, the law would not stop her, borders and governments would not stop her, insults would not stop her, religion would not stop her, ethnicity would not stop her, people's perception of her would not stop her—she came to be blessed and she knew Jesus had power to heal her baby. And when he saw her faith, not her hair, not her nationality, not her clothes, not her accent, but her faith . . . he had to respond and he healed her daughter, and the direction of his ministry changed completely. His direction changed and his love poured out on this woman and on all of us. Who let the dogs in? Jesus did, and when he did he included me.

It's time for the dogs—those who are pushed to take the dirty left-over bread that the privileged have thrown on the floor—the dogs—to stand up, speak up, and move up to the table. The church desperately needs you.

The dogs change the direction of the church by bringing us back to what matters and away from the ritualistic, religious, and traditional junk that keeps people from Jesus. The dogs change the direction of the church by their pure faith. Dogs say things like, "Let's be clear. You may disagree with my:

> profession,
> recovery,
> relationship,
> how or if I pay bills,
> how or if I clean my house,
> whether I do or don't exercise,
> how I raise my children;

but you cannot keep me from the grace of Jesus, no matter what fresh difficulties you placed in my way." Thank God for the dogs.

Pentecost—making Jesus available to all—will come again if the dogs show up. The responsibility to usher in the New Pentecost does not rest on traditional religious folks. They will never change anything because the current system is comfortable for them. Dogs keep the church honest.

The future of the church belongs to the dogs . . . it always has. Get up, dogs, and get to Jesus! Open up the way so the church can see once again the all-encompassing love of God in Jesus Christ!

OVERCOMING FEAR-BASED RELIGION

Hebrews 12:18–29

> Indeed so terrifying was the sight (of Mount Sinai) that Moses
> said, "I tremble with fear." But you have come to Mount Zion
> and to the city of the living God, the heavenly Jerusalem, and
> to innumerable angels in festal gathering . . . (Heb. 12:21–23)

FEAR IS GENERATIONAL and hard to get under control. Our families and
communities tell us what and whom to fear and then we add to it for
generations following. "Don't let so-and-so people fix your car. Don't
ever get into a business relationship with so-and-so. Keep your boys
away from so-and-so." Religion is a major culprit because it includes supernatural retribution to control our behavior: "Jesus will get little girls
who steal candy. God will strike you blind if you do that." People whom
we consider religious often attack us, and because we believe in and fear
God, our relationship with God is often fear-based.

Fear is institutional and a very useful tool in the hands of a nation
or a government that knows how to use it. The formula is that any response of our government or institution, no matter how violent, is jus-
tifiable to secure our safety and the safety of those we hold dear. The in-

stitution simply has to create a villain so heinous that such a response seems warranted. You can see the process of creating a villain in any action film, and by the end of the movie our sainted mothers will call for the villain's blood if the scriptwriter and the actor can make him or her look evil enough in the earlier scenes.

Fear is controlling and it holds creative, innovative, and effervescent people hostage . . . particularly if there is someone to point to who tried and failed at what we are attempting. "See what happened to Jim when he stepped out . . . the same thing will happen to you if you take that risk." We listen, we stop, the years go by, we regret it, and we despair.

Mount Sinai represents fear. Many of us were trained to associate God and religion with fear. Listen to the words that describe Mount Sinai.

Gloomy darkness, tempest or whirlwind, fire or multiple lighting flashes—a terrifying place thought of as the habitation of God. The voice of God is described as so frightening and awesome that the people begged that God talk to Moses only and then Moses could tell them what God said. This was not a description of a relational loving God.

These images invoke thoughts of the history of Christianity— crusades, inquisitions, hangings, blood, burnings, excommunications, and trials by drowning, slavery, the subjugation of women, and the abuse of same gender loving people. It reminds us of Bible-based manifest destiny and patriarchy, black clothes and starched shirts, starched skirts and starched hearts . . . selfish piety with no regard for or kindness to those who are different. I see images of Afghani and Iraqi mothers crying for mercy for their children to the same God the American mothers cry to.

People have done frightful things because they cowered under the wrath of a frightful God.

Look now to the words that describe Zion. Zion symbolizes the place where the Christ reigns, the place where grace is victorious over legalistic fear-based religion. Zion is the safe home for the believer. There is protection in the company of angels, fellowship in the general assembly of the people of God, witnesses both living and dead, and Jesus the advocate and mediator who stands against all who accuse us. His death, his blood is not seeking revenge like Abel's, but rather it is shed for our redemption and reconciliation.

You would think that if people could move from such a dreadful place as Sinai to a place of confidence, assurance, and joy like Zion, that they would do it straightaway; but it seems that the fearmongers are also powermongers who capitalize on the need of the fearful to be afraid of God. I call it a form of spiritual masochism. It follows the classic model of spousal abuse where there is plug and a socket. And it is big business too, but all smoke and mirrors. As people move toward relationship with a loving God, they are less likely to fall victim to "God handlers" who use God as a violent pit bull under their command.

But notice the balance of the chapter that suggests that a shaking is coming so that the things that cannot be shaken will be revealed and will remain. Let us remember with godly and relational reverence that we have received a reign of God that is full of grace and not terror and we are obligated to free ourselves from religious tyranny and then to set about freeing others. When I fly on commercial airplanes the flight attendant mantra includes a piece that says, "In case of a loss of cabin pressure, oxygen masks will drop down . . . put your mask on first, then assist children and those in need of your assistance." Encourage yourself first and then encourage all people to think, and not to check their brain at the door of the church. Encourage yourself and others to vote with your feet, if you are under oppressive fear-based theology.

If you are on Sinai, move. If you look back and see others still there, tell them to move. When you hear our nation's religious and political leaders using fear to pass laws and snatch freedoms hard won, tell them fear only begets fear . . . we are a people of faith who speak truth to power until change comes. Our foundation is faith, not fear; love, not revenge. Who wins if we kill people who kill people and become killers to show killers that killing is wrong?

Martin Luther King Jr. said this: "I refuse to accept the cynical notion that nation after nation must spiral down a militaristic stairway into the hell of thermonuclear destruction. I believe that unarmed truth and unconditional love will have the final word in reality. This is why right temporarily defeated is stronger than evil triumphant . . ."[1]

Choose Zion . . . the air is clear up here.

THE BODY OF CHRIST

1 Corinthians 11:17–34

> When you come together, it is not really to eat the Lord's
> supper. For when the time comes to eat, each of you goes
> ahead with your own supper, and one goes hungry and an-
> other becomes drunk . . . do you show contempt for the
> church of God and humiliate those who have nothing? . . .
> (Jesus) said, . . . "Do this in remembrance of me." . . . So then,
> my brothers and sisters, when you come together to eat, wait
> for one another. (1 Cor. 11:20–21, 22b, 24b, 33)

THERE CAN TRULY BE NO LORD'S SUPPER, no communion, no Holy
Eucharist in a community whose members do not love each other. We
may as well call it a poorly planned dinner party.

There were divisions among the Corinthian saints. Some were authentic and some were not. The comportment of authentic believers exposed those who used Christianity for personal, economic, or political
purposes (v. 18–19).

Several things were wrong with the supper, due in large part to the
stratification of the Corinthians.

There were private separate networking parties going on. Class and social status separated people. Those who could get off early or did not have to work rushed to eat the best food and drink the best wine before the others arrived.

Many were left humiliated, possibly because they were excluded from the meal entirely, or because they did not have the means to contribute to the lavish preparations, and felt guilty partaking of the meal.

It was a mockery of the common meal, initiated by Jesus, designed to be accessible to all, in remembrance of him. The meal was to commemorate an act of love by sharing in love with one another (1 Cor. 10:16–17). Authentic remembering was to imitate Christ, not just to have a dinner in his honor. The meal was to bring the high down and the low up until they were one in Christ.

Paul gave a warning, "Be careful how you take this supper."

Paul had in mind the lack of loving concern that the Corinthians had for one another. He told them if they partook in the supper unworthily they classed themselves with those that murdered Jesus. He then recommended the importance of self-examination, leading to reconciliation with God and each other, prior to participation in the supper. He was encouraging the Corinthians to evaluate the authenticity of their relationship to others in the body of Christ. *You must properly discern the Savior's body.* They were coming together supposedly to honor Jesus' body and all the while they were abusing it. They did not know who is really included in the body of Christ.

Beloved, we are the body of Christ. You cannot celebrate the Savior's body if you do not love and take care of the whole body. Why is the church sick and feeble? Why is the church of little effect in critical times? Because the hand is saying to the foot, I don't need you . . . touch is what is important. The eyes say to the stomach, I don't need you . . . seeing is all that is essential to the body.

The church at Corinth did not discern the Savior's body. The church of today still does not discern it. Class, denominations, political affiliation, race, nationality, gender identification, and affectional orientation separate us, and we use the church and the name of Jesus to reinforce these divisions and barriers. And because of this, our influence is weak, sick, and in some cases dead.

Paul suggests a remedy to bring the church back to a real remembrance of what authentic communion embodies. Verse 33 says when you come together for the supper, wait for one another. I recall when I was about eleven or twelve my family determined that I was the best candidate to travel with my maternal grandmother on a trip to see my aunt in Seaside, California. We had a number of major mishaps . . . we bought tickets to the wrong city, my grandfather ran over my grandmother's alligator shoe as he pulled off, the lady in front of my grandmother leaned back too far and my grandmother pushed her up into her ice cream cone, the bags went on to the wrong city, while my truly "sanctified" grandmother and I waited for my aunt in a very smoky, dimly lit Spanish-speaking roadside bar. It was the trip from hell.

We finally got to my aunt's house, and I huffed and puffed the bags inside and sat down to rest, at which time my grandmother requested that I run yet another errand. Well, I had had it and I protested, letting my grandmother know how unjust it was for her to ask me to do another thing. My protestations were out of character for me, as we just didn't say certain things to my grandmother, and while I was protesting I looked for closest escape route. Her response was also out of character. She said, "Yvette honey, it is a privilege for you to 'wait on' me." I didn't see it that way then, but now as she sleeps in Jesus, I agree. It was a profound privilege for me to "wait on" my grandmother.

Paul tells the Corinthian saints to wait for each other. This implies that everyone has a right to be a part of the supper, although we are not all in the same place at the same time. We don't all see things the same. We don't all believe things exactly the same. We can wait for each other. Some of us go fast and some take a little time. We can wait for each other. We don't all have the same balances in our bank accounts, but the table of Jesus is for all of us. Some of us are mourning the loss of yesterday and afraid of tomorrow. We can wait for each other. We can hope and believe that those who say cruel things today will say kind things tomorrow. We can wait for each other. I must bear with you and you must bear with me. We can't give up on one another, for we are all the body of Christ and we can wait for each other.

The New War

Jeremiah 29:11, Romans 12:21

"For surely I know the plans I have for you," says the LORD, "plans for your welfare and not for harm, to give you a future with hope." (Jer. 29:11)

Do not be overcome with evil, but overcome evil with good. (Rom. 12:21)

OUR SCRIPTURE OPENS during a grim time in the history of Israel. They are in captivity to Babylon. They have had their temple and all things sacred to them ransacked and desecrated. Their most brilliant people have been conscripted to work for the enemy on threat of death. Their God has been displaced and their enemies are mocking them. They have ceased to sing Zion songs and have hung their harps on willow trees in this strange land. There is no singing for joy . . . just lamenting. It is particularly difficult because they have never experienced this kind of desolation, this threat to their national security and spiritual stability before. They thought themselves spiritually insulated from their enemies. What they thought could never happen, happened.

Additionally there is an abundance of "I told you so" prophets who are always on hand to give the same basic word. Essentially they repeated the theme, "When we were in prosperity it was because we were pleasing God and being obedient. Now that we are suffering it is because we are not pleasing God and God is beating us up." I know this was an especially hard word for Israel to hear from the theological spin-doctors who always use the pain and fear associated with disaster to promote themselves as true oracles of God after the fact. The same kind of bad theology is being preached in the aftermath of the events of September 11, 2001. Shame on anyone who would use their pulpit, mailing list, or television program to further inflict pain of this disaster by suggesting God's wrath has fallen on these innocent people from all walks of life, because of the "sins" of the nation . . . and then use this event to justify a vendetta war against an unrelated regime. Even if God were as punitive and vengeful as religion and nations can be, it would seem God would specifically eliminate those who fit the "sin" category and take revenge on the actual perpetrators without collateral damage.

I believe today we can imagine the loss Israel must have felt much more closely because of the loss we have recently experienced. The events of September 11, 2001, and the aftermath beg the question. Where is God in the midst of all of this?

It is far too simple to say that this painful and horrific loss of September 11 is a result of America no longer being a "B" movie. Remember Pearl Harbor happened when abortion was illegal, there was prayer in school, women, gays and blacks were in their "place," and we were allegedly a pure Christian nation. Pearl Harbor happened when America was just what some televangelists say they want it to be again. Additionally we must ask, "Are all countries and people who suffer terrorism and injustice evil? Is suffering the result of God's anger and wrath? Are we objective enough or informed enough to determine who is right and who is wrong?"

Who is right?

The Hutu or the Tutsi in Rwanda?

The Protestants or the Catholics in Ireland?

The Jews or the Palestinians in Israel?

U.S. imperialism or Iraqi oppression?

What happened on September 11, 2001, has but one source and that source is our common enemy. Evil. The fact that evil visited our country should come as no great surprise to us. We are a relatively new player in the world, and it took some time for this kind of evil to get to us, but we are not exempt. Evil has visited many more mothers and fathers, sons and daughters, husbands and wives, spouses and partners . . . many of whom love their families and love God just as we do. And even though terrorism of this kind and magnitude is new to us, we have used terrorism against our selves and others for years.

The KKK and white supremacist groups are terrorists.

Those who blow up abortion clinics are terrorists.

Those who promote violence against SGL people and transgenders are terrorists. Spousal abusers and those who support the physical and emotional abuse of women and children are terrorists. Those that would use their power to destroy programs for the poor to benefit the rich are terrorists. Those who have closed the borders of this nation to immigrants are terrorists.

The spread of HIV/AIDS to more than thirty million souls is largely due to the religious and societal terrorism of shame, guilt, and denial. We know about terrorism. Many of us perpetrate it. Many of us are victims of it.

But terrorism comes from evil, not from God. This is not the hand of God working to bring harm. In the midst of Israel's suffering and loss God speaks and tells them where God's heart is for them. No matter what religion says, God says: "For surely I know the plans I have for you, . . . plans for your welfare and not for harm, to give you a future with hope" (Jer. 29:11).

This is where God's heart is for us today. This is where God's heart is for all of creation. Suffering will come. As long as evil exists, suffering will come. The miracle is in how God and God's people step up during this time. We can overcome evil with good. This is the time to put down the atmosphere of evil with good. We can overwhelm evil—cancel out its effect with good. Justice does not mean retaliation. Find something extraordinarily good to do, some senseless act of kindness and generosity. This will keep us off of the endless treadmill of "tit for tat" or an eye for an eye. No one wins in that atmosphere and evil gains strength.

Where is God in the midst of this? God is at the intersection of our marginality. Too long have the forces of evil sought to separate us and make us spend too much energy fighting for our special interests. I am calling for a revolution—people of color, fighting for freedom with and for same gender loving people of every race. Elderly people standing with the youth of our nation. The poor and the immigrant and the undereducated working together for common goals. God is working at the junction of our combined marginality. You see, no one is home until all of us are home. God is working through people of faith who have declared their houses of worship "hate free zones" open to all people. God is working through people who are giving time, money, blood, food, and clothes. God is working through people marching for peace and decrying war. God is everywhere. God is here working among us, enlightening us, planning our future . . . and our future is full of hope.

Broken Cisterns

Jeremiah 2:13

> For my people have committed two evils: they have forsaken
> me, the fountain of living water, and dug out cisterns for
> themselves, cracked cisterns that can hold no water. (Jer. 2:13)

JEREMIAH, THE PROPHET TO JUDAH, in giving cause to Israel's fall into
Babylonian captivity, spoke to some things very inherent in human nature.

Judah was not ignorant of the blessing of living water in an arid
land. Water was in short supply in many places most of the year. This
was a dusty, dry, hot place. Underground springs and streams or wadis
that flowed or bubbled up with fresh, life-giving water were considered
more valuable than gold. People could drink, and the flocks could drink,
without fear of disease. Fresh water cleaned itself in the flowing or bub-
bling process. Far too often, however, fresh water was not available and
large stone pots were either fashioned and buried in the soil or were dug
right into the rock to hold rainwater. This method of water supply was
problematic because the standing water would soon become home to
various insects, bacteria, harmful algae, and other organisms that often
brought disease and death to humans and animals. Cistern water was

often reserved for necessity—drinking or cooking, not bathing, as it was in short supply.

This makes Jeremiah's illustration all the more poignant. Why forsake a fountain of living water and dig out for yourself a cistern that isn't even a good cistern, and be thirsty and dirty? Why give up something for nothing?

A recent television special examined the question of happiness. It studied people who had won lotteries and inherited money to see if it brought happiness. As you can imagine, the sudden influx of much money wreaked havoc in most of their lives. Distrust of people, broken relationships, entitlement issues with family members, worry about investments, and such had made them less happy. So what brings happiness? A test was done to see what made babies happy. A string was tied to the baby's hand and the other end to a switch that turned a colorful picture off and on. Soon the baby got the concept and was thrilled with this newfound ability to pull the string and get the picture. When the researchers disabled the switch the baby became visibly frustrated but when they started intermittently flashing the picture without the use of the switch, the baby had a fit. What was it that made the baby so happy initially? It wasn't the picture alone, it was *control*.

The spring of living water is under God's control. The cistern is mine. I dug it out. I decide where it will be placed. I decide who can use it. I decide how much water everyone can have. "They dug out cisterns for themselves." Something that is dead looking like something alive when the something alive is available. But to have living water we must be dependent on God. Dead things can be organized and controlled, like in a museum of stuffed animals and bones. Much can be learned there about our origins—about what we used to be—but a dead thing can never take the place of the living.

I believe some Christians, churches, and denominations are on life support—still breathing but for all intents and purposes dead. Living solely on what *was* said, written, done, and given. Why should I seek to support this ministry? We have enough endowment to live on. Why should I seek to hear from God? I can read and listen to what others have said and let that suffice. Besides, if I have to live by faith, write songs or sermons by faith, build by faith, raise children by faith, change jobs by faith, wait on the right companion by faith I will be unhappy because I'm not in control. No, I'd rather have something dead I can control than something alive where anything is possible. And so we perpetuate things that do not work—things that are dead but have been sanctified by time.

When I was growing up we had a sister in the church who took care of the youth department. She was a wonderful jovial person who was extremely effective with children . . . but she could not cook. I mean she could not cook, period. She was the kind of cook who, when she fried chicken, it was red at the bone and burned on the outside. Her cake was too salty and doughy at the center . . . she could not cook. However, she raised more money that any department when she sold dinners after church. People would give her a donation for the youth in place of buying the dinners, and we kids would eat the food, and cut around the raw and uncooked portions. We loved it when she was in the kitchen. But as I look back I realize that I never knew a time when this sister ever baked a good cake. And it begs the question, "What is a twenty-five-year-old bad cake"? *A bad cake!* Time does not change a bad cake into a good one, only changing the ingredients can do that.

Bottom line: If we want a living way that remains relevant and flowing we must be prepared to admit that our cisterns are substandard, broken, and without life. We must give up control, stop requiring that everyone continue to eat bad cake, and start asking God to show us living water. There is no science to it. That is why it is so difficult. Why did Israel so often leave Jehovah for other gods? Because they could see them and move them around the house: *control*. Control of gods with no power is an exercise in futility. A life fully surrendered to the living God is a well of fresh water. There is an old Pentecostal song my grandmother and mother used to sing that says, "We ought to stop planning some time and let God have his way." The way of God is the way to life.

MOTHER MARY

Luke 1:26–31

> In the sixth month the angel Gabriel was sent by God to a town
> in Galilee called Nazareth, to a virgin engaged to a man whose
> name was Joseph, of the house of David. The virgin's name was
> Mary. And he came to her and said, "Greetings, favored one!
> The Lord is with you." But she was much perplexed by his
> words and pondered what sort of greeting this might be. The
> angel said to her, "Do not be afraid, Mary, for you have found
> favor with God. And now, you will conceive in your womb and
> bear a son, and you will name him Jesus." (Luke 1:26–31)

DO NOT BE AFRAID . . . how can she not be afraid? This pregnant teenager
in a patriarchal warring society? She like so many women is threatened
with stoning for babies born out of wedlock, as if by an unholy ghost.

Do not be afraid—yeah, right—with this sudden chaotic change in
her life. Now she has to deal with being considered spoiled and damaged goods in a culture where her virginity is her only real commodity.

Where will she go and to whom will she turn? She thinks of
Elizabeth, her cousin/mother with the "yes" face. This girl in trouble

needs an Elizabeth, a refuge, and a welcoming presence glad for a new life no matter how it got there. Elizabeth, who herself was pregnant with the promise of God.

Why did Mary choose Elizabeth? There had to be something in the past that made her know her cousin would offer solace and understanding. Maybe Elizabeth had a warm kitchen with the smells of fresh bread and a ready ear for troubled souls. Perhaps other young women found their way to her with the religious hounds on their trail.

What a splendid reputation Elizabeth had . . . one you can go to in trouble.

Elizabeth took hold of Mary with work-worn hands, took hold of her tenderly and said the things that built her up for what was to come. Elizabeth kept Mary close for three months, as long as it took to fortify Mary for what was ahead.

So great was this love and support that it took Mary through birthing in a stable, being a refugee in Egypt, being rejected by her home town, watching her son move closer and closer to his destiny, giving him direction, loyally supporting him, yet fearing for his life . . . because he was special, so he was vulnerable.

She could not protect him from his destiny. Every confrontation with the status quo brought him closer to his death; and she knew, as mothers do, that it was bigger than the both of them.

Yet remembering the love-support of her cousin/mother brought Mary comfort and strengthened her resolve even in her darkest hour, and she stood firm while her son Jesus was afflicted and accused, arrested, tried, and executed.

You see, when the words "do not be afraid" come from someone who loves you and holds your heart, the words have the power to bear you up and hold you tightly even when you would and should lose your mind.

And Mary went on to become the first church mother full of faith and power, sharing with others Elizabeth's words to her . . .

Blessed are you among women and blessed is the fruit of your womb . . . blessed is whatever the Holy Spirit has impregnated you with; blessed is your vision; blessed is your purpose; blessed is your ministry; blessed is your fruit, whether you are a young one like Mary or a aged one like Elizabeth; blessed are you who have believed in the promise of God!

CONCLUSION

THERE ARE MANY MORE GROUPS and individuals who could have been used as examples of people on the visible margin. However, I felt compelled to write about some of the more difficult issues facing the communities where I have and do currently serve. The locus of my experience is primarily among African Americans in the inner city, but there are margins surrounding every community and there is an overwhelming need to take church to the edge rather than seeking to bring the margin to the center. The edge is where Jesus did his best work, but most mainstream Christians fear it deeply. In 1901 James Bryce, the British historian, wrote about the United States during the time when African Americans were thought to epitomize the edge. Fear of the "other" speaks through his words:

> The presence of the blacks is the greatest evil that threatens the United States. They increase, in the Gulf States, faster than do the whites. They cannot be kept forever in slavery, since the tendencies of the modern world run strongly the other way. They cannot be absorbed into the white population, for the whites will not intermarry with them, not even in the North where they have been free for two generations. Once freed, they would be more dangerous than now, because they would not long submit to be debarred from political rights. A terrible struggle would ensue.[1]

Sadly, this kind of misplaced apprehension and fear still exists.

Africans were taken from their homes and brought to the Americas by force. In relationship to the effect of slavery on the African, Noel Erskine writes, "Tremendous damage was done to the personality of the Black person when he or she was forced to live outside the indigenous community. Existence-in-relation sums up the pattern of the African way of life."[2] African slaves were from one continent but many tribes, speaking many languages and representing many cultures. Yet in spite of their diversity, their common bondage and need for a healing community encouraged them to create common bonds: communities on the margin. After a while the many tribes became the African American community. There is a quote from the slave narratives that epitomizes how community was created on the margins of slavery and what they did when they grew tired of oppressive theology:

> The preacher came and. . . . He'd just say, "Serve your masters. Don't steal your master's turkey. Don't steal your master's chickens. Don't steal your master's hawgs . . . same ole thing all the time. My father would have church in the dwelling houses and they had to whisper . . . that would be when they wanted to have a real meeting with some real preaching . . . they used to sing their songs in a whisper and pray in a whisper. That was a prayer meeting from house to house—once or twice a week.[3]

The groups discussed in this book are also separated from their communities of origin, driven out by those who fear those they do not understand. Their common oppression creates common bonds, a common need for affirmation, and a common need for community.

All humans need community. According to Peter Paris, "African Americans have always known that persons cannot flourish apart from a community of belonging."[4] It is extremely important that community be created among marginalized people due to the real distance between people on the edge and their communities of origin. Paris states, "[African Americans] have also known that any community that oppresses its members is no community at all but, rather, a seething cauldron of dissention, distrust, and bitterness."[5]

People who are oppressed by the church must be empowered to develop communities separate from the mainstream or their faith in a

God of Justice will be severely damaged by the continual attack of their oppressor. One cannot thrive in an atmosphere of moral contradictions where the love of God and hatred of the "other" or the stranger is preached simultaneously. Where these moral contradictions exist, there remains the potential of the victim becoming the victimizer, just to survive. This oppressive theology is contagious. Racism is wrong. Homophobia is wrong. The people who have been victimized by prejudice must decry it and establish communities that labor to love.

I have identified some groups truly marginalized by church and society and suggested some methods and theology for creating, sustaining, and celebrating community on the margin. Additionally I have shared my thoughts, experience, and passion regarding preaching on the edge along with some sermons and teaching materials—all of this because my heart is committed to the mission of seeing the radically inclusive love of Jesus Christ visibly, tangibly, and palpably demonstrated in the earth.

When I think of creating, sustaining, and celebrating Christian community on the margin, I am reminded of a documentary on volcanoes, which showed the power that exists just below the surface of this planet. Volcanoes have shaped this planet and have given us our island paradises, warm springs, and geysers. However, they also have the power and potential to erupt, disturb, and reshape everything as we know it. Such is the passion and power of a group of people in crisis grouped together with no pretenses and an earthshaking faith in God. Although there exists the potential for destruction if the passion is not channeled, if care is taken, the power can be harnessed for the good of the community.

This is a story without a conclusion, as it is still being written and celebrated through the lives of an emerging community who thought they could never have a seat at the table. "It does not yet appear what we shall be," or what new, prophetic, and powerful results will come from the next eruption. I pray for a day when no one will be made to feel he or she is not good enough to have a seat at God's table, but in the interim I will advocate for strong, affirming faith-based communities established by marginalized people firmly planted on the edge of church and society. Just as new land emerges from the mouth of a volcano creating fresh possibilities, so emerging Christian communities must rise up with power and purpose. "What shall we say to these things? . . . If God be for us who can be against us!" (Rom. 8:31).

TWELVE STEPS: THE REFUGE RADICAL INCLUSIVITY MODEL[1]

Working Assumptions for Faith Communities to Create, Sustain, and Celebrate Community on the Margin

ONE

Radical inclusivity is and must be radical.

In its effort to be inclusive the church often reaches out carefully to the margin. Radical inclusivity demands that we reach out to the farthest margin, intentionally, to give a clear message of welcome to everyone.

TWO

Radical inclusivity recognizes, values, loves, and celebrates people on the margin.

Jesus was himself from the edge of society with a ministry to those who were considered least. Jesus' public ministry and associations were primarily with the poor, weak, outcast, foreigners, and prostitutes.

THREE

Radical inclusivity recognizes harm done in the name of God.

Many people rejected by the church got their burns from Bible-believing Christian flamethrowers. Contempt for the church and all things religious often stems from exposure to oppressive theology, biblical literalism, and unyielding tradition.

It is neither Christ-like nor spiritual to be oppressive. No human being is born with a destiny to be oppressed or to oppress others.

FOUR

Radical inclusivity is intentional and creates ministry on the margin.

"On purpose," because of the radical inclusive love of Jesus Christ, the inclusive community deliberately makes a conscious and unapologetic decision to love and celebrate the Creator's diversity, welcoming all persons regardless of race, color, ancestry, age, gender, or affectional orientation. Radical inclusivity practices and celebrates the Christian community outside of the dominant culture, believing that the realm of God includes the margins of society and is a perfect place for ministry. Marginalized people, now as in the time of Jesus' earthly ministry, respond to a community of openness and inclusivity, where other people from the edge gather. Such an atmosphere welcomes people to feel safer to be who they are.

FIVE

Radical inclusivity's primary goal is not to imitate the mainline church.

The true church belongs to God and is the body of Jesus Christ; it cannot be owned exclusively by any denomination, person, or group. Further, adherence to religious dogma is not freedom. There are wrongs in organized religion due to oppressive theology, bibliolatry, and some traditional beliefs, which prevent freedom for all people and which we can never fully right. Radical inclusivity, however, is ministry rooted in restoration—believing that God has given the church the work and ministry of reconciliation and using the power of love to model and demonstrate the radically inclusive love of Jesus Christ.

SIX

Radical inclusivity requires a new way of seeing and a new way of being.

"From this day forward, we regard no one from a strictly human point of view, not even Jesus" (2 Cor. 5:16). This scripture passage implies that we can celebrate one another in some new and powerful way in Christian community—some way that both accepts who each of us is in a human sense and transcends our humanity, allowing us to see each other as God sees us. Christian community can truly be celebrated when we realize the church is a spiritual, mystical, faith community and we relate best when we make the drop from head to heart.

SEVEN

Radical inclusivity requires awareness, information, and understanding.

The creation of Christian community among people marginalized by the church requires that the community be prepared and maintain a presence of cultural familiarity through education and training, which equips the community to understand, actively fight, and overcome oppressive and exclusive theology and practices. Sustaining and eventually celebrating community on the margin requires the church to reexamine relational ethics, develop a theology of radical inclusivity, and destigmatize its view of any group of people.

EIGHT

Radical inclusivity does not hide and works to undo shame and fear.

The radically inclusive ministry of Jesus does not encourage people to hide their "unacceptable" realities (based upon the dominant culture's point of view or faith) in order to be embraced. True community comes when marginalized people take back the right to fully "be." People must celebrate not in spite of who they are, but because of who their Creator has made them. In order for marginalized people to have community they must develop community "naked" or exposed with their "marginality" in full view while often celebrating the very thing that separates them from the dominant culture.

NINE

Radical inclusivity recognizes diversity on the margin.

People live and are located on the various margins of society for many different reasons. Most people live on the margin because the dominant culture and/or faith communities have forced them outside their boundaries to a margin. Not all marginalized people are poor, uneducated, or visible. Because most marginalized people are together on the margin does not mean that each affirms the other or that their common marginality will hold the community together.

TEN

Radical inclusivity must be linked to preaching and teaching.

The creation of Christian community among people marginalized by the church requires preaching and teaching that defines and strengthens the essence of the community through a theology of radical inclusivity. Preaching and teaching defines, reinforces, and supports the collective theology of the community.

ELEVEN

Radical inclusivity demands hospitality.

Marginalized people experience hospitality where they have neither to defend nor to deny their place or their humanness. Real hospitality agrees with the notion and acknowledges the fact that everyone already has a seat at the welcome table of God—all they need do is claim it.

TWELVE

Radical inclusivity is best sustained and celebrated when everyone in the community is responsible and accountable.

Sustaining Christian community requires an intentional effort to design a framework that includes everyone in the life of the church. The dissemination of duties and tasks ensure that all members share in and contribute to the welfare of the community. It is often difficult for people who have not had continuity in life to understand that freedom without responsibility and accountability is as detrimental as slavery. Freedom cannot be an end unto itself. Freedom from something must flow into freedom to be something else or it is not truly freedom. The object of getting free is being free: the object of being free is living free.

Notes

INTRODUCTION

1. Letty M. Russell, *Church in the Round: Feminist Interpretation of the Church* (Louisville: Westminster John Knox Press, 1993), 25.

2. SGL—same gender loving—is used as a term inclusive of gay, lesbian, bisexual, and queer persons.

3. Albert Memmi, *The Colonizer and the Colonized* (New York: Orion Press, 1965), 9.

CHAPTER 1

1. Loren B. Mead, *Five Challenges for the Once and Future Church* (Bethesda, Md.: The Alban Institute, 1996), 44.

2. Jung Young Lee, *Marginality: The Key to Multicultural Theology* (Minneapolis: Fortress Press, 1995), 86.

3. Peter J. Gomes, *The Good Book: Reading the Bible with Mind and Heart* (New York: William Morrow and Company, 1996), 51.

4. Methodist/Baptist/Pentecostal

5. Peter J. Paris, *The Spirituality of African Peoples: The Search for a Common Moral Discourse* (Minneapolis: Augsburg Fortress, 1995), 62.

6. John L. Kater, *Christians on the Right: The Moral Majority in Perspective* (New York: Seabury Press, 1982), 116–17.

7. Quoted by Edgard Legare Pennington, in *Thomas Bray's Associates and Their Work Among the Negroes* (Worcester, Mass.: American Antiquarian Society, 1939), 25.

8 John B. Cade, "Out of the Mouths of Ex-Slaves," *Journal of Negro History* 20 (July 1935), 329.

9. M. Shawn Copeland, "Wading Through Many Sorrows," in *A Troubling in My Soul*, ed. Emilie Townes (Maryknoll, N.Y.: Orbis Books, 1993), 124.

10. Delores S. Williams, "James Cone's Liberation: Twenty Years Later," in James H. Cone, *A Black Theology of Liberation: Twentieth Anniversary Edition* (Maryknoll, N.Y.: Orbis Books, 1990), 189–90.

11. Elias Farajaje-Jones, "Breaking Silence: Toward an In-the-Life Theology," in *Black Theology: A Documentary History, Volume Two, 1980–1992*, ed. James H. Cone and Gayraud S. Wilmore (Maryknoll, N.Y.: Orbis Books, 1993), 141.

12. A. Leon Higginbotham, *Shades of Freedom* (New York: Oxford University Press, 1996), 37.

13. Stephen Carter, *Reflections of an Affirmative Action Baby* (New York: Harper-Collins Publishers, 1991), chapter 8.

14. Gary David Comstock, *Unrepentant, Self-Affirming, Practicing: Lesbian/ Bisexual/Gay People within Organized Religion* (New York: Continuum Publishing, 1992), 190.

15. Gary David Comstock, *Gay Theology without Apology* (Cleveland: Pilgrim Press, 1993), 92.

16. Donald M. Chinula, *Building King's Beloved Community: Foundations for Pastoral Care and Counseling with the Oppressed* (Cleveland: United Church Press, 1997), 2.

17. Ibid.

18. Gomes, *The Good Book*, 36.

19. Kater, *Christians on the Right*, 80.

CHAPTER 2

1. Martin Luther, "The Freedom of the Christian," in *Martin Luther: Faith in Christ and the Gospel*, ed. Eric W. Gritsch (Hyde Park, N.Y.: New City Press, 1996), 105.

2. Kater, *Christians on the Right*, 98.

3. Welsh Neck Baptist Church Minutes, 1738–1932. "American Negro Slavery," excerpted in Mullins, ed., typescript, South Carolina Library, University of South Carolina, 278–80.

4. Michael S. Piazza, *Rainbow Family Values: Relationship Skills for Lesbian and Gay Couples* (Dallas: Sources of Hope Publishing, 1995), 43.

5. Betty Berzon, *Permanent Partners: Building Gay and Lesbian Relationships That Last* (New York: Plume/Penguin Group, 1988).

6. Ibid., 9.

7. Robert Bellah, "Evil and the American Ethos," lecture sponsored by the Wright Institute at Grace Cathedral, San Francisco, February 22, 1970, 3.

8. Karen Lebacqz, *Professional Ethics: Power and Paradox* (Nashville: Abingdon Press, 1985).

9. Ibid., 76.

10. William N. Eskridge, *The Case for Same-Sex Marriage: From Sexual Liberty to Civilized Commitment* (New York: Simon & Schuster, 1996), 8–9.

11. Linda Handel, *Now That You're Out of the Closet, What About the Rest of the House?* (Cleveland: Pilgrim Press, 1998), 95.

12. Ibid.

13. Margaret A. Farley, *Personal Commitments: Beginning, Keeping, Changing* (San Francisco: Harper Collins, 1986), 64.

14. Reinhold Niebuhr, *Moral Man and Immoral Society* (New York: Touchstone, 1932), 81, 257.

15. Proposition 187 was designed to limit government-supported human services to persons who are undocumented and have alien status. Proposition 209 was designed to eliminate government-supported affirmative action programs.

16. Carolyn Lochhead, "The Third Way," in *Beyond Queer: Challenging Gay Left Orthodoxy*, ed. Bruce Bawer (New York: Simon & Schuster, 1996), 52.

17. Robert N. Bellah, et al., *The Good Society* (New York: Vintage Books, 1991), 217–19.

18. Martin Luther King Jr., from the speech, "I Have a Dream," August 28, 1963, Washington D.C. Bracketed phrase mine.

19. Bellah, *The Good Society*, 217–19.

20. Sharon D. Welch, *A Feminist Ethic of Risk* (Minneapolis: Fortress Press, 1990), 104.

21. Mary Ann Tolbert, "Reading for Liberation," in *Reading From this Place Vol. 1: Social Location and Biblical Interpretation in the United States*, ed. Fernando F. Segovia and Mary Ann Tolbert (Minneapolis: Augsburg Fortress, 1995), 275–76.

22. John Shelby Spong, *Living in Sin?: A Bishop Rethinks Human Sexuality* (San Francisco: Harper Collins, 1988), 79.

23. Theodore Walker Jr., *Empower the People: Social Ethics for the African-American Church* (Maryknoll: Orbis Books, 1991), 63.

24. Robert Williams, *Just as I Am: A Practical Guide to Being Out, Proud and Christian* (New York: Harper Collins, 1992), 211.

25. Ibid., 208.

26. Gordene Olga MacKenzie, *Transgender Nation* (Bowling Green, Ohio: Bowling Green State University Popular Press, 1994), 14.

27. Leslie Feinberg, *Transgender Warriors: Making History from Joan of Arc to RuPaul* (Boston: Beacon Press, 1996), 12.

28. Edmund White, *States of Desire: Travels in Gay America* (New York: Plume, 1991), chapter 2. Transvestite often refers to cross-dressers.

29. Kory Martin-Damon, "Essay for the Inclusion of Transsexuals," in *Bisexual Politics: Theories, Queries, & Visions,* ed. Naomi Tucker (New York: Harrington Park Press, 1995), 246.

30. Intersexuality is a set of medical conditions that features "congenital anomaly of the reproductive and sexual system." That is, a person with an intersex condition is born with sex chromosomes, external genitalia, or an internal reproductive system that is not considered "standard" for either male or female.

31. John Shelby Spong, London: *Daily Telegraph,* July 12, 1990.

32. Spong, *Living in Sin,* 79.

33. Marcel Reich-Ranicki, tr. 1989, *Thomas Mann and His Family* (London: Collins, 1987).

34. Charlotte Elliott, "Just As I Am," 1835, verse 3.

35. Keith Boykin, *One More River to Cross: Black and Gay in America* (New York: Doubleday, 1996), 173.

36. Homophobia is fear of homosexuality. Homohatred is abhorrence of homosexuals and homosexuality. Heterosexism is discrimination against homosexuals that provides heterosexuals disproportionate power and privilege.

37. *The Impact of Homophobia and Other Social Biases on AIDS* (San Francisco: Public Media Center, 1995), 5.

38. Ibid., 12.

39. James Baldwin, "Freaks and the American Ideal of Manhood," *Playboy* 32, no. 1 (January 1985), 150–51, 192, 256–60.

40. Christine Smith, *Preaching as Weeping, Confession, and Resistance: Radical Responses to Radical Evil* (Louisville: Westminster John Knox Press, 1992), 88.

41. Ibid., 99, 108.

42. Ibid., 101.

43. Ann Thompson Cook, "And God Loves Each One: A Resource for Dialogue About the Church and Homosexuality," Reconciling Congregation program, 1988, Nashville, 13.

CHAPTER 3

1. John and Arline Liggett, *The Tyranny of Beauty* (London: Gollancz, 1989).

2. John Darnton, *Neanderthal* (New York: Random House, 1996).

CHAPTER 4

1. This chapter previously appeared as "Managing the Thorn," a chapter I contributed to Jana Childer's *Birthing the Sermon* (St. Louis: Chalice Press, 2001).

2. Henry H. Mitchell and Emil M. Thomas, *Preaching for Black Self-Esteem* (Nashville: Abingdon Press, 1994), 133.

3. Fred B. Craddock, *Preaching* (Nashville: Abingdon Press, 1985), 27.

4. David Buttrick, *A Captive Voice: The Liberation of Preaching* (Louisville: John Knox Press, 1994), 30.

5. Lenora Tubbs Tisdale, *Preaching as Local Theology and Folk Art* (Minneapolis: Fortress Press, 1997), 57.

6. Craddock, *Preaching*, 164.

7. Frank A. Thomas, *They Like to Never Quit Praising God: The Role of Celebration in Preaching* (Cleveland: United Church Press, 1997), 5.

8. Richard Ward, *Speaking from the Heart: Preaching with Passion* (Nashville: Abingdon Press, 1992), 48–49.

9. Ibid.

CHAPTER 19

1. Martin Luther King, Jr., Nobel Prize acceptance speech, Oslo, Norway, December 10, 1964.

CONCLUSION

1. James Bryce, *Studies in History and Jurisprudence* (New York: Macmillan, 1901), vol. 1, chapter 6.

2. Noel Leo Erskine, *King Among the Theologians* (Cleveland: Pilgrim Press, 1994), 173.

3. George P. Rawick, general ed., 1936–38, *The American Slave: A Composite Autobiography*, supplement series 1, vol. 8 Arkansas Pt. 1 (Westwood, Conn.: Greenwood Publishing, 1977), 35.

4. Paris, *The Spirituality of African Peoples*, 117.

5. Ibid.

APPENDIX

1. A teaching tool I wrote that was adapted to the twelve-step format by Rev. Valerie Brown-Troutt.

Glossary*

Androgynous person: An androgynous person may identify and appear as neither clearly male nor female or as between male and female.

Cross dressers: Formally known as transvestites, cross dressers identify and are completely comfortable with their assigned birth gender. To varying degrees, they take on the clothing and mannerisms of the opposite gender for emotional fulfillment. They may do this either publicly or privately.

Gender expression: Refers to the ways in which people externally communicate their gender identity to others through behavior, clothing, hairstyle, voice, and emphasizing, de-emphasizing, or changing their body's characteristics. Gender expression is not necessarily an indication of sexual orientation.

Gender identity: One's internal sense of being male or female. One's gender identity can also innately reside somewhere in between or outside the boundaries of the binary expression of male or female.

Heterosexism: The belief that everyone is or should be heterosexual.

Heterosexual: A person who is emotionally and sexually attracted to members of the opposite gender.

Heterosexual privilege/heteronormativeness: Cultural, societal, and religious/theological systems that support the rights and privileges that heterosexuals enjoy and SGL persons often do not. Examples of these privileges include legal protection, public shows of affection, acceptance in certain religious communities, and the like.

Homophobia: The irrational fear and hatred of SGL persons and same sex love that often includes a systematic oppression of SGL individuals and their culture.

Internalized homophobia: When a SGL person believes and accepts cultural, societal, and religious/theological prejudices about SGL people and same sex love.

Intersexed: Formally known as hermaphrodites, intersexed persons are born with some degree of physical ambiguity regarding their gender.

Same gender loving (homosexual): A person who is emotionally and sexually attracted to members of the same gender.

Sex assignment surgery (also gender reassignment or gender confirmation surgery): A series of surgeries for transsexual people and intersexed people. For female-to-male transsexual it may involve removal of the breasts and the reconstruction of the chest, removal of the internal female reproductive organs, and occasionally the creation of a phallus. For male-to-female transsexuals it involves the surgical construction of the vagina and sometimes breast implants, facial reconstruction, and other surgeries. For intersexed persons surgery may involve correcting the errors made by doctors with regard to gender.

Sexual orientation: One's affectional, emotional, psychological, and sexual attraction.

Transgender: An umbrella term for people whose gender identity or expression does not conform to the cultural norm for the gender into which they were born, or the sex that they were assigned at birth.

Transphobia: The irrational fear and hatred of transgender and transsexual people. A systematic oppression of transgender individuals and their culture.

Transsexual: Denotes a person born into one gender but who identifies physically, psychologically, and emotionally as the opposite gender.

*Parts adapted from training designed by Yosenio V. Lewis and Moonhawk River Stone. Permission to use is granted, provided full credit is stated. Additional contributions from Ashley Moore.